AEIILRTTVY

Bob Szantyr

2011

Afterword by Jesse Bransford

ISBN 978-0-615-71180-5

1920 -11 -11 -9 -8 -7 -5 -2 0 0 0 0 1 1 1 1.7 2 2 2 2 2 2 2 2 3 3.14 5 6 6 6 7 8 11 11 15 18 20 20 21 26 30 43 43 109 520 1919 1919 1920 2002 300,000 - ! ! ! !, !, & ((((((((((Êther-drift (true) (uniform (World) (World) (1) (1) (1) (1). (10), (10). (10a) (10a). (11). (11a) (11a) (11a). (12) (12). (1920; (2! 2R3). (2) (2) (2) (2). (2). (3) (3), (3). (4), (4). (5) (5), (5), (5), (6) (6), (7a), (7b) (8) (8) (8a) (8a) (8a). (9), (9). (a (a (a) (a) (a) (a) (a) (a) (a) (A) (A) (aberration), (acceleration), (and (and (and (and (and (and (approximately) (arcs (as (as (as (at (at (Authorised (away (axioms) (b) (b) (b) (b) (b) (B) (B) (b) (B) (B), (because (body (Bonn), (Brazil), (c) (c) (c) (centrifugal (cf. (Cf. (Cf. (Cf. (chest). (considered (co-ordinales) (coordinate (co-ordinate (co-ordinate (co-ordinate (co-ordinate (coPart (December, (developed (Die (directed (distance) (Doppler (during (e.g. (e.g. (e.g. (e.g. (e.g. (e.g. (e.g. (e.g. (Eddington, (electrons) (embankment) (Euclidean) (event) (events) (expanding (F) (Fig. (finiteness) (for (for (Force) (Force) (formulation (formulation (from (Galileian (Galileian) (Galileian) (Gaussian (Gaussian (Gaussian (gravitational (here (here (http//www.gnu.org/licenses/fdl.txt). (I (i.e. (i.e. (i.e. (i.e. (i.e. (i.e. (i.e.really)with (if (in (in (in (in (in (in (in (in (in (in (in (in (in (in (in (indefinitely (indistinguishable (inertial (intensity (K) (K0) (large) (Leverrier (line-interval) (line-interval), (line-interval).Bychoosingonecornerofasquareas (lit. (lit. (lit. (M/r), (marxists.org) (mollusc) (N.B. (non-rotating) (not (not (of (of (or (or (or (or (or (or (position (possessing (railway (realised (really (reference-body (referencebody) (relative (relative (relativity (results (retardation) (retardation) (Riemann, (rigid (rod (S) (Section (Section (Section (see (see (similar (simultaneous (special) (special) (sup. (sup. (sup. (Supplementary (supplementary (Supplementary (surface) (t1 (the (the (the (three-dimensional) (time) (uni-dimensional) (unique)co-ordinatesystemtooccasiontheintroductionoftheÊtheridea, (v (v) (West (what (which (with (world), (x (x (x' (x' (x' (x) (x, (x1=0) (x2),even),thatthespectrallinesemittedshowedaredshiftwhichincreased).

') .) . A c o - ordinatesystemKthencorrespondstothe)hashadanimportant)ofspacecausedbythesun.)ofspaceisindependentoftime. , , , , , ,Euclidean . . . ., ; ? ? ? ? ? ? ? ? ? ? ? ? ? ? ? ? ? [A] [A] [A] [A] [British] [first [in [Note [Note] [see _ _ _ _ _ _ _ _ _ _, _, _- rays _t1 _t1 _x _x' _x' +43 = © 0 0 0), 0, 0. 01. 01. 02. 02. 03. 03. 04. 04. 05. 05. 06. 07. 08. 09. 1) 1) 1) 1) 1) 1) 1) 1) 1) 1) 1) 1) 1) 1) 1) 1) 1) 1) 1) 1) 1) 1) 1) 1) 1) 1) 1) 1) 1) 1)), 1, 1. 1.08.1027; 10 10. 100 101 102 103 104 105 106 107 108 109 11 11) 11) 11). 11. 110 111 112 113 114 115 12 12, 12, 12, 12. 126-129). 13 13 13. 132) 14 14. 15 15. 16 16. 17 17) 17) 17. 17. 18 18 18. 1859; 1895) 19 19. 1916 1916 1916 1916) 1919, 1919. 1924, 1924. 1999, 2 2 2 2 2 2 2 2 2 2 2 2 2 2 2 2! 2) 2) 2) 2) 2) 2) 2) 2), 2, 2, 2. 2/k 20 20 20. 21 21, 21. 21; 22 22 22. 23 23 23 23). 23). 23, 23. 24 24. 24. 25 25 25. 26 26, 26. 27 27. 28 28. 29 29. 29th 29th 2g12dudv 2g12dx1dx2 3 3) 3) 3) 3, 30 30 30. 30. 31 31. 32 32) 32) 32. 33 34 35 35, 36 3600. 37 38 39 4 4!R2 4!R2. 4) 40 41 42 43 43 44 45 46 47 48 48), 49 5 50 51 52 53 54 55 56 57 58 59 6 6 6 6, 6, 6. 60 61 62 63 64 65 66 67 68 69 7 7) 7) 70 71 72 73 74 75 76 77 78 79 8 80 81 82 83 84 85 86 87 88 89 9 90 900) 91 92 93 94 95 96 97 98 99 a a a A A a A A A A a a a A a a a a a a A a a a a A a a a A a a a a a a a a a a a a a a a a a a A a a a a a a a a a a a a a a a a a a a a a a a a a a a a a a a a a a a a A A a a a A a a a a a a a a a a a a a a a a a a a a A a a a a a a a a a a a a a a a a a a a a a a a a a a a a a a a a a a a a a a a a a a a A a a a a a a a a a a a a a a a a a A a a a A a a a a a a a a a a a a a a a A a a a a a a a a a a a a a a a a a a a a A a a a a a a a a a a a a a a a a a a a a a a a a a a a a a a a a a a a a a a a a a a a a A a a a a a a a a a a a a a A a a a a a a a a a a

A a a a a a a a A a a a a a a a a a a a a a a a a a a a a a a
a a a a a a a a a a a a a a a a a a a a a a a a a a a a a a a
a a a a a a a a a a a a a a a a a a a a a a a a a a a a a a a
a a a a A a a a a a a A a a a a a a a a a a a a a a a a a a a
a a a a a a a a a a a A a a A a a a a a a a a a a a a a a a a
a a a a A a a a a a a a a a a a a a a a a a a a a a a a a a a
a a a a a a A a a A a a a a a a a a a a a a a a a a a a a a a
a a a a a a a a A a a a a a a a a a a a a a a a a a a a a a a
a a a a a a a a a a a a a a a a A a a a a a a a a a a a a a a
a a a a a a a a a a a a a a a a a a a a a a a a a a a a a a A
a a a a a a a a a a a a a a a A a a a a a a a a A a a A a a a a
a a a a a a a a a a a a a a a a a a a a a a a a a a a a a a a
a a a a a a a a a a a a a a A a a a a a a a a a a A a a a a a
a a a a a a a a a a a a a a a a a a a a a a a a a a a a a a a
a a a A a a a A a a a a a A a a a A a a a a a a a a a a a a a
a a a a a a a a a a a a a a a a a a a a a a a a a a a a a a a
a a a a A a a a a a a a a a a a a a a a a A) A, A, A, A, A, A. A. A. A. A. A. A. a. A1 A1 AB AB AB. AB. abandon able able able able able able able able able able able able able able able able able able able able about, above above above above above above above above above above above above above above above above above above, above, above, above. above. above. abscissa abscissa absent absent. absent. absolute absolute absolute absolute absolute, absolutelyatrest, absorbed absorbs absorbs abstract abstract abstract abstraction accelerated accelerated accelerated accelerated accelerated accelerated accelerated accelerated accelerated accelerated accelerated acceleration acceleration acceleration acceleration acceleration acceleration acceleration, acceleration, acceleration, acceleration. accelertion accented accented accept acceptance accepted access accompanying accompanying accord accord accord, accordance accordance accordance accordance

accordance accordance accordance accordance accordance accordance accordance accordance accordance accordance accordance according According according According According According According according according According according according according according According According According According According According according according According according According according according According According according according According according according according according according According according according according according according according According according according according according according According according according according according according according according according according according according according according account account account account account accuracy accuracy accuracy accuracy accuracy, accurately, accustomed accustomed achieved acknowledge, acquaintance acquaintance acquainted acquired across acting action action action action action action action action action actions acts acts acts actual actual actual actual actual actual actual actually actually actually ad Adams Adams add add added added added added adding addition Addition addition Addition Addition Addition addition addition addition addition addition, additional additional adhere adhere adhered adjacent adjacent adjacent Adjacent adjacent adjacent adjust adjustments admit admit admit admit admit admit, admits advance advance advance advances advances advancing advantageous advent advent advent advisable Êther Êther Êther Êther, Êther. Êther. Êther. Êther-drift Êther-drift Êther-drift, affects affords afore-mentioned Africa) After After After after After after after after After after after again again again again again again again again again again, against against against against against against against against agency ago ago, ago, agree agreement agreement agreement agreement agreement agreement agrees agrees ahead aid aid aid aid aid aid aid, Aided aims air air air aiso Albert

Albert alike all all all all all all all all all All all all all all all all all all all all all all all all all all all all all all all all all all all All all all all all all all all all all all all all all all all all all all all all all all) all, all, Allbodies AllGaussianco-ordinatesystemsareessentiallyequivalentfortheformulation all-inclusive allotted allow allow allow allowed allows alluded almost almost almost almost alone along along along along along along along along along along along along along along along along along alongside alongside already already already already already already already already already already already already already already already already already already also also also also also also also also also also also also also also also also also also also also also also also also also also also also also also also Also also also also also also also also also also also also also also also also also also also also also also also also also also also also also also also also also also also. alteration alteration alteration alterations altered altering alters although although although Although Although always am am am am am am am am among amongst amongst amount. amounted amounts amounts an An an an an an an an an an An an an an an An an an an an an an an an an an an an an an an an an an an an An an an an an an an an an an an an an an an an an an an an an an an an an an an an an an an an An an an an an an an an an an an an an an an an an an an an an an an an an an an an an an an an an an an an an an an an an an an an an an an an an an analogous analogous analogous analogous analogous analogous analogous analogously Analogously, analogy, analyse analyse analysis analytical analytical and And and and and and and and and and and and and and and and and and

and and and and and and and and and and and and and and and and and And and and and and and and and and and and and and and and, and, and/or angle angle angle angle angle angle angular angular anisotropic annular another another another another another another another another another another another another another another another another another, another, another, another, another. another. another. another. answer answer answer answer answer answer answer answer answer answer answer answer answer answer, answered answering anxiety any any any any any any any any any any any any any any any any any any any any any any any any any Any any any any any any any any any anyone anyone anywhere Apart apart apart. apartofthetwoeventsorfour-dimensionalpoints. apparatus apparatus. apparent Apparent Apparent apparent apparent apparent apparent apparent apparently apparently appeals appear appear appear appear appear appear appear appear appear appear appearance, appeared appeared appeared appears appears appears appears appears appears appears, Appendices Appendix appendix Appendix Appendix Appendix Appendix Appendixes appertaining applicability applicable application application application application application application application applied applied applies applies applies applies apply apply apply apply apply applying appreciable appreciably appreciably appreciate appreciate approach approach approach approaches approaches appropriate appropriately approrimately approximately approximation approximation approximation approximation. arbitrarily arbitrarily. arbitrary arbitrary arbitrary arbitrary arbitrary arbitrary arbitrary arbitrary arbitrary, arc arc arc arc arc) arc. arc. Archive Are are are are are are are are are are are are are are are are are are are are are are are are are are are are are are are are are are are are are are are are are are are are are are are are are are are are are are are are

are are are are are are are are are are are are are are are are are are are are are are are are are are are are are are are are are are are are are are are are are are are are are are are are are are are are are are are are are are are are are are are are Are are are are are are are are are are are are are are are are are are are are are are are are are are are are are are are are are are are are are are are are are are are are are are are are are are are are are are are are are are are are are are are are are are are are are are are are are area area area area area area area, arena. argument argument argument argument Argument argument, arguments arguments arise arise arise, arise. arises arises arises arises around around aroused arranged arranged arranged arranged arrangement arrangement arrangement arrangement arrangement arrangement. arrive arrive arrive arrive arrive arrive arrived arrived arrived arrived arrived arrow as as as as as as As As as As as as as as as as As as As as As as as as as as as as as as as as as as as as as as as as as as as as as as as as as as as as as as as as as as as As as as as as as as as as As as as as as as as as As as as As As as as as As as as as as as as as as as as as as as as as as As as as as as as as as as as as as as as as as as as as as as as as as As as as as as as as As as as as as as as as as as as as as As as as as As as as as as As as as as as as as as as as as as as as as as As as as as as as as as as as as as as as as as as as as as as as As as As as as as as as as As as as as as as as as as as as as as As as as as as As as as as as as as As as As as as as as as as as as as as as as as as as as as as as as as as as as as As as as as as as as as as as as as as as as as as as ascertained ascribed ask ask ask ask ask ask ask ask ask asking asks assertion assertion assertions asserts assign assign assign assign assigned assigned assigned, assignment, associate associate associate associated associated associated associated associated association assume assume assume assume assume

assume assume assume assume assumed assumed assumed assumed assumed assumes assuming assuming assumption assumption assumption assumption assumption assumption, assumption, assumption, assumptions assumptions assumptions assumptions assumptions, astonished astonished, astoundingly astronomer astronomer astronomers astronomers astronomers astronomers astronomers.1) Astronomical astronomical Astronomical astronomy astronomy astronomy, astronomy, At at At at at at at At at at at at at at at at at at At at at at at at at at at at at at at at at at at at at at at at at at at at at at at at at at at at at at at at at at at at at at at at at at at at at at at at at at at at at at at at At at at at at At at at at at at at at at at at At at at at at at at at at at at at at at at at at at at At at at at at at at at at at at at at at at at at at at at at at at at at at at at at at at at at, at. atmosphere atom atom atom atom atom). atrest atrest. attach attach attach attached attached attached attached attached attached attached attached attached, attaches attaching attain attainable attainable attained attempt attempt attempt; attempted attempts attempts attempts attending attention attention attention attention attention, attenuated attracted attracting attraction attraction attraction attraction attractive attracts attribute attribute attribute author authorised auxiliary avail available available available available available, average average average average average average average average, awakened away away, ax axe axes axes axioms, axioms. axioms. axioms. axis axis axis axis B b B B B B B B B B B B B B B B B b B B B B B B) B) B, B, B. b. B. B1 B1 Bachem back backwards bands, basal base based based based based based based based based based, Basgen basis basis basis basis basis Basis basis basis basis basis basis basis Basis basis basis basis basis basis basis. BC be

be be be be be be be be be be be be be be be be be be be be be
be be be be be be be be be be be be be be be be be be be be be
be be be be be be be be be be be be be be be be be be be be be
be be be be be be be be be be be be be be be be be be be be be
be be be be be be be be be be be be be be be be be be be be be
be be be be be be be be be be be be be be be be be be be be be
be be be be be be be be be be be be be be be be be be be be be
be be be be be be be be be be be be be be be be be be be be be
be be be be be be be be be be, beam beam beam bears bears beautiful beauty became became became became because because because because because because because because Because because because because because because because because because Becauseitisattractedbytheearth. become become become become become becomes becomes becomes becomes becomes becomes becomes becomes, becoming been been been been been been been been been been been been been been been been been been been been been been been been been been been been been been been been been been been been been been been been been been been been been been been been been been been been been been been been been been been been been Before before Before Before before before before before before before Before before before before before Before before. before. begin beginning beginning) begins behave behave behave behaves behaviour Behaviour behaviour Behaviour Behaviour behaviour behaviour behaviour behaviour behaviour Behaviour behaviour behaviour behaviour behaviour behaviour behaviour behaviour behaviour behaviour behaviour behaviour behaviour being, beings beings beings beings beings beings beings beings beings beings beings believe believe believed believes believes believes belong belongs belongs belongs belongs Berlin). best best best better between

between between between between between between Between betweenneighbouring beyond biology, bluish bluish bluish bodies bodies bodies bodies bodies bodies bodies bodies bodies bodies bodies bodies bodies bodies bodies bodies Bodies bodies bodies bodies bodies bodies bodies bodies bodies bodies bodies, bodies, bodies. bodies. bodies. bodies. bodies. bodies. bodies.1) Body body body body body body body body body body body body body body body body body body body body body body body body body body body body body body body body body body body body body body body body body body body body body Body body body body body body body body body body body body body body body body body body body body body body body body body body body body body body body body). body, body, body, body, body, body, body, body. body. body. body. body. body. body. body. body. body. body. body. body. body. bodyofreference Boltzmann, book book book book book, book, book. book. book; borrowed both Both both both both both both both both both both both both both both both Both Both both bottomless bounds. brake, brakes) brakes, branch Brian brief briefly briefly briefly briefly, brilliant brilliant bring Britain's broad broad brought brought brought brought build building built built. business But But But But But but But But but But But But But But But But But but But But but but but But But But but but But but But But but But but but But But But but but But but But But but But but but But but but but but but But but But but but but But but But But but but But but but But But but But but but but But but But but But but But but but but but but but but but but but but but But but but But but but but But but, But, But, But, but, by by By By by by By by by by By By by by by by by by by by by by By by by by by by by by by by by by by by by by by by by by by by by by by by by by by by by by by by by by by by by by by by by by by by by by by by by by by by by by By by by by by by by by By By by by by by by by by by by by by by by by by by by by by by by by By by by by by by by by by by by by By by by by by by by by by by by by by by by by by by by by By by by by by by by by by by by by by by by by by by By by by by by by by by by by by by by by by by by by by by by by by by by by by by by by by by by by by by by by by by by by by by by by by by by by By by by by By by by by by by by by By by by by by by by by by by by by by by by by by by by by by By by by by by by by by by by by by by by by by by by by by by by by by by By by by by. C C c c c c c c c C C C c C c c, c, c, c. c. c. c. c. c. c. C.G.S. c= c2dt1 c2dt2 c2dt2, c2t2 c2t2 c2t2 c2t'2 c2t'2 c2t'2 c2t'2 c2t2) calculate calculate calculated calculation calculation calculation calculation calculation) calculation, calculation, calculation, calculations call call call call call call call call call called called called called called called called called called called calling calls came can Can can can can can can can can can can can can can can can can can can can can can can can can can can can can can can can, cannot canservation capable capable capable capable capable capable capable capable caprice, care care care, careful careful careful carefully carefully carefully. carriage) carriage) carriage, carriage, carriage, carriage, carriage,

carriage, carriage, carriage, carriage, carriage, carriage, carriage. carriage. carriage. carriage. carriage. carriage. carriage. carriage. carriage. carriage. carried carried carry carry carry Cartesian Cartesian Cartesian Cartesian Cartesian Cartesian Cartesian Cartesian Cartesian Cartesianco-ordinates Cartesianco-ordinatesystem case case case case case case case case case case case case case case case case case case case case case case case case case case case case case case, case, case, case, case, case, case, case, case. case. case. cases cases, cases. cast cast catalogue. cathode cause cause cause cause cause cause cause cease ceiling celebrated celestial celestial cent. central central central centre centre centre centre centre centre centre centre centre centre centre centre centre centre centre centre centre, centre. centre. centrifugal centrifugal century century century, century, century. certain certain Certain certain certain certain certain certain certain certainly certainly certainly certainly certainly certainly certainly certainty certainty, Cf. Cf. ch ch ch. change change change changed changed changes changes changes changing changing character character character character character characterise characterise characterise characterise characterised characteristic characteristic characters. charm chased chest, chest. child child choice choice choice choice choice choice choose choose choose choose choose choose choose choose choose, choose, chosen chosen chosen chosen chosen chosen chosen chosen chosen chosen. chosen. chosen. circle circle circle circle circle circle circle circle circle, circle, circle. circle. circle. circles circular circular circular circular circular circular circular circumference circumference circumference circumference circumferenceoftheuniverse circumstance circumstance circumstance circumstance, circumstances claim claim claim claimed claims class classes Classical classical classical classical classical Classical classical Classical classical Classical classical classical classical Classical classical classical classical classical classical

classical classical Classical classical classical classical Classical classical classical classified clear clear clear clear clear clear clear clear clear clear clear clearer clearly clearly clearly clearly clearly clearly clearly clearly clearness clearness clearness, clearness, clearness, clock clock clock clock clock clock clock clock clock clock clock clock clock clock clock clock clock clock, clock, clock, clock. clocks clocks clocks Clocks clocks Clocks clocks Clocks clocks clocks clocks clocks clocks clocks Clocks clocks clocks clocks clocks clocks clocks clocks clocks clocks clocks clocks clocks clocks clocks, Clocks, clocks, clocks, clocks. clocks. close close close closed closed closed closed closure clothes. cloud cloud cloud cloud cloud. cloud. Co co co- cobbler. coincide coincide coincide. coincidence coincidence coincidence coincides coincides coincides coincides coincides. collected colour colour colours colours, combination combine combined combined come come come come come come come come comes comes comes comes comes coming coming coming coming commissioned Committee committing common common common common. common-place companion comparable comparatively compare compared compared compared compared compared compared compared compared compared compared compared compared compared compared compared compared compared compared comparison comparison comparison comparison comparison comparison Comparison comparison. comparison. comparison. compass compasses. compatible compelled compelled compelled compensate compilation complete complete complete complete complete completed completely completely complex complicated complicated complication components components composed comprehensibility comprehensive comprehensive comprehensive conceivable conceivable. conceive concept concept Conception conception conception conception conception conception Conception conception conception, conception, conceptions conceptions conceptions concerned concerned concerned concerns concervation conclude conclude conclude conclude, concluded conclusion conclusion conclusion conclusion conclusion conclusion conclusion

conclusion conclusion conclusions conclusions conclusively conclusiveness condition condition condition condition condition condition condition condition condition condition condition condition condition condition condition condition, condition, condition. conditions conditions conditions conditions conditions, conditions, conditions. confine confirmation Confirmation Confirmation confirmed confirmed confirmed confirmed confirmed confirmed. conflict conflict conflict conflict conformable conformable conformably confronted confronted confused conjunction conjunction conjunction connected connected connected connected connecting connection connection connection connection connection connection connection connection connection connection connection connection connection connection connection conscience conscientious conscientiously consequence consequence consequence consequence consequence consequence consequence consequence consequence consequence consequence consequence consequence, consequence, consequence, consequence, consequence. consequently conservation conservation conservation conservation conservation conservation consider consider consider consider consider consider consider consider consider consider consider consider consider, considerable considerable considerable considerable, considerably considerably considerably consideration, consideration, consideration, consideration. consideration. consideration. consideration. consideration. Considerations considerations considerations considerations considerations Considerations considerations considerations Considerations Considerations Considerations Considerations Considerations Considerations Considerations Considerations considerations considerations

considerations considerations considerations considerations considerations considerations considerations considerations considerations considerations considerations considerations considerations, considerations, considerations, considerations, considerations. considerations. considerations. Considered considered considered considered considered considered considered considered considered considered considered Considered considered considered considered considered considered considered, considered, considered, considered, considered. considered. considering consist consistent consistent, consists constancy constancy constancy constancy constancy constancy constant constant constant constant constant constant constant constant constant constant constant constant constant constant constant constant constant constant constants constants constants constants constants constitute constitute constitute constitute constitute constituted constitutes constituting constituting constrained constrained constrained constrained construct construct construct constructed constructed construction construction construction construction construction construction construction construction construction construction, construction, construction. constructions constructions constructions constructions contain contained contained contained contains contended contended content Contents contintium continua continua, continua. continually continue continue continue continued continues continues continues continuity; continuous continuously continuously continuously continuously continuum continuum continuum Continuum Continuum Continuum continuum continuum continuum Continuum continuum Continuum Continuum continuum Continuum Continuum continuum continuum continuum Continuum Continuum continuum continuum continuum continuum continuum continuum continuum continuum continuum continuum continuum continuum continuum continuum continuum continuum continuum continuum continuum, continuum, continuum, continuum, continuum, continuum. continuum. continuum. continuum. continuum. continuum. continuum. continuum. continuum. continuum; contracted contraction

contraction contraction contraction contraction contraction contradict contradictory contradictory contrary, contrary, contrary, contrary. contrast contrast contrast contrast contributed convenience convention conversant conveys conviction conviction conviction convince convince convinced convinced convinced convincing, convincingly coordinate coordinate coordinate coordinate coordinate coordinate coordinate coordinate coordinate coordinate coordinate co-ordinate coordinate) co-ordinate, co-ordinate. co-ordinate. coordinates coordinates coordinates coordinates coordinates coordinates coordinates coordinates coordinates co-ordinates Co-ordinates Co-ordinates co-ordinates co-ordinates Co-ordinates co-ordinates co-ordinates co-ordinates co-ordinates Co-ordinates co-ordinates co-ordinates co-ordinates Co-ordinates co-ordinates Co-ordinates coordinates) coordinates) co-ordinates). coordinates, coordinates, co-ordinates, co-ordinates, coordinates. coordinates. coordinates. coordinates. co-ordinates. co-ordinates. co-ordinates. co-ordinates. co-ordinates. co-ordinates. co-ordinates. co-ordinates. co-ordlnates copy Copyleft copyright corner corner corner corner corner, correct correct correct correct, corrected correctly correctly correctly, correctly, correctness correctness correctness. correlates correspond correspond correspond correspond correspond correspond correspond correspond correspondence corresponding corresponding Corresponding corresponding corresponding corresponding corresponding corresponding

corresponding corresponding corresponding corresponding corresponding corresponding corresponding correspondingly corresponds corresponds corresponds corresponds corresponds corresponds corresponds corresponds corresponds corresponds Cosmological Cosmological cosmological cosmological cosmological cost Cottingham, could could could could could could could could counter-point counter-points course, course, course. co-variant covers covers covers criterion Crommelin, crucial crystallised ct ct ct ct' ct' ct) ct) ct) ct') ct') ct'). ct, ct1 curvature curvature curvature curvature curvature curvature curvature curvature. curve curve curve, curve. curved curved curved curved curves Curves curves curvilinear curvilinearly customary cut c-v. cyanogen D1, D2, dare dark Darwinian data data data data data, data, Davidson), day, day. days De deal deal deal deal dealing deals deals dealt deceived December, December, decide decide decided decided decides deciding decision decision decision decisive. declare decreases decreases deduced deduction deduction, deduction. deductions deductions deductions deductions deductions deductions deductions deductions, deductive deep deeply defect defect; defects define define define defined defined defined defined defined defined, defined. defining definite definite definite definite definite definite definite definite definite definite definite definite definite definitely definitely definition definition definition definition definition definition definition definition definition definition definition definition definition definition definition definition definition), definition). definition, definitions definitions Deflection deflection deflection deflection deflection deflection degree degree degree delicacy delicacy delicacy delicacy demand demanded demands demands demands demands demands demonstrate demonstrate denote denote dense dense density density density density density density density density density density. departed departs depend depend depend depend depend dependence dependent

dependent dependent dependent dependent depends depends depends depicted derivable derivable derivable derivation Derivation Derivation derivation derivation derive derive derived derived derived derived derived derived derived derived derived derived derived derived descend describe describe describe described described described described described described described describes describes describing describing describing description description description description description description description description description description description description description description description description description description, description, description. description. description; designate designate designate designated designated designating desire despite despite despite destined destiny detail detail detail detail detail detail detail detail detail, detailed detailed detailed detailed detect detectable. detected detecting detecting detection. determine determine determine determine determine determine determine determine determine determine determined determined determined determined determined determined determined determined determined determined determined. determines determines determines determining detour develop developed developed developed. development development development development development development development development development development development development, develops deviate deviated deviations deviations deviations. devised devised devoid devoted diagonals diagonals diagonals, diagram diagram diagram diagram, diagram. diagram. dials. diameter diameter diameter, did did did did did did did differ differ differ differ differ differ differ differeace difference difference difference difference difference difference difference difference, differences differences differences differences). differences, differentials differentiate differently differing differing differs differs differs differs difficult difficult difficult difficult difficult difficult difficulties Difficulties

Difficulties difficulties difficulties difficulties difficulties. difficulties. difficulties? difficulty difficulty difficulty difficulty difficulty difficulty difficulty difficulty difficulty difficulty difficulty difficulty difficulty, difficulty. difficulty. dilemma dilemma dilemma, dimensional dimensional dimensional dimensions dimensions dimensions. dimensions. dimensions. dimensions. diminish diminish, diminished diminishes diminishes diminution dimishes direct direct direct directed direction, direction, direction, direction, direction. direction. directions directions. directions. directions. directly directly directly directly directly directly directly directly. directly; disagreement disappearance disappearance disappears disappears, disappears. disc disc disc disc disc disc disc disc disc disc disc disc disc disc disc disc disc) disc, disc, disc, disc, disc, disc, disc, disc, disc, disc, disc, disc, disc, disc. disc. disc. discard discarded, disclose discover discovered discovered discovered discovering discovers discovery discrepancies discuss discuss discussed discussed discussed discussed discussed. discussing discussion discussion discussion discussion discussion discussion discussion discussion, discussion, discussion, discussion. disdain disdainful disorder displaced displaced displacement displacement displacement Displacement displacement displacement displacement displacement displacement displacements displacements displacentent disposal disproved. disregard disregard disregard disregarding dissatisfied distance distance distance distance distance distance distance distance distance distance distance Distance distance Distance distance, distance, distance, distance. distances distances distances

distances distances distances, distances; distant distant distasteful distinguish distinguishable distribute distributed distribution distribution disturb disturbing diverge divide divided dividing division, do do do do do do do do do do do Do do do docks document Documentation does does does does does does does does does does does does does does does does does does does does does does does does does does does does does does does does does does does does doing doing doing). domain domain domain domain domain domain domain domain domain domain domain domain domain, domains domains domains, done done Doppler's double doubt doubt doubt doubt doubt, doubted doubted doubtless doubtless down down down down downwards. draw draw draw draw draw draw draw draw drawing drawn drawn drawn drawn, drop drop drop dropped ds ds ds. ds2 ds2 ds2 ds2 ds2 ds2 ds2 dt. dt1. du du, du2 due due due due due duration duration, during during during during During during during during during during during during during during dust. Dutch dv dv, dv2 dx, dx1 dx1 dx1 dx1, dx2 dx2 dx2 dx2 dx3 dx3 dx4 dx4 dy, dy1 dy1, dy2 dy2 dz dz1 dz1, dz2 dz2 E e E. E. e.g. e.g. e.g. e.g. E0 E0 E0 E0, E0. Each each each each each each each each each each each each each each each each each each each each each each each each each each each each each each each each each each each each each earlier earlier earlier earlier early earth earth earth earth earth earth earth earth earth earth earth earth earth earth earth earth earth) earth, earth, earth, earth, earth. earth. earth. earth. earth's easily easily easily easily easily easily easy eccentrically eccentricity, eclipse eclipse eclipse eclipse eclipse eclipse eclipse eclipse. eclipse-photograph Eddington edge edge edge edition education effect effect effect effect effect effect effect effect effect effect effect effect effect effects effects effects efforts Einstein Einstein Einstein Einstein Einstein Einstein EINSTEIN Einstein

Einstein either either either either elapses electric electric electric electrical electrical electrical electrical electrical electricity. electrified electrodynamic electrodynamical electrodynamical electrodynamical electrodynamics electrodynamics electrodynamics electrodynamics electrodynamics electrodynamics electrodynamics electrodynamics electrodynamics electromagnetic electromagnetic electromagnetic electromagnetic electromagnetic electromagnetic electromagnetic electromagnetic electron electron electron electron electron electron electron. electrons electrons, electrostatic electrostatics Electrostatics electrostatics elegance elegance elegantly element element eliminate ellipse ellipse ellipse ellipse ellipse ellipse ellipse, ellipse, ellipse, ellipsoid) elliptical elliptical) elliptical). ellipticalspace. else else else else else emancipation embankment) embankment) embankment) embankment). embankment). embankment, embankment, embankment, embankment, embankment, embankment, embankment, embankment, embankment, embankment. embankment. embankment. embankment. embankment. embankment.

embankment. embankment. embankment. embankment. embraces emerged emission emission emits emits emitted emitted emitted emitted emitted emitted emitted emitted emitted emitting emitting emphasised empirical empirical empirical empirical empirical empirical empirical empirical empirical empirical empirical empirical empirical employ Employed employed employed emptiness. empty empty empty enable enables enables enclose encounter encounter encounter encounters encounters encounters encounters. end end end end end end end end end endeavour end-points ends ends ends energies energy, energy. energy. energy. engaging English enlightened enough enough ensure ensure ensured enter entered enterprise enterprise. enters enters enters entertain entirely entirely entirety) entitled epitome epitomised epoch-making equal. equality Equality Equality equality equality equality equally equally equally equation, equation. equation. equations, equipped equipped equipped equivalence equivalent equivalent equivalent equivalent equivalent equivalent. equivalent. equivalent. erected. erecting error, errs escape escape escape especial Especially especially essence essential essential essential essentially essentially essentially establish establish established Established estimated estimated etc., etc., etc., etc., etfect Euclidean Euclidean Euclidean Euclidean Euclidean Euclidean Euclidean Euclidean Euclidean

Euclidean Euclidean, Euclideancontinuum. Euclid's Even even even even even even even even Even even Even even even even even even even event, event, event. event. events Events events, events, events, events, eventually ever Evershed every Every every Every every every every every every Every every every every Every every every every every every every every Every every Every every Every every every every every every every every every every every every every every every every every every everyday everyone everything everywhere everywhere everywhere everywhere everywhere, everywhere, evidence evidence evidence evident evident evident evident evinced. evolution evolved exact Exact Exact exact exact exact exact exact exact exact exact exact exact exact. exactly exactly exactly exactly exactly exactly exactly exactly exactly exactly exactly exactly exactly exactly exactly exactly exactly exactly exactly. exactly. exactly. exactness exactness exactness examination examination examination examination, examine examine examining example example example example example, example, example, example, example, example, exceed exceeded exceedingly exceedingly exceedingly exceedingly exceedingly exceeds excellent excels excels exception exception exciting exclude exclusive exclusively exclusively executing executing executing exerted exhibits exhibits exist exist exist exist, exist, existence existence existence existence existence existence existence existence existence existence existence existence existence existence, existence, existence. existing exists exists exists exists exists exists exists exists exists exists

exists, exists. expand expand, expanding expansion expansion expansion expansive expect expect expect expect, expected expected expeditions expeditions Experience Experience Experience experience experience experience experience experience experience experience experience experience experience experience experience experience experience experience experience, experience, experience, experience, experience, experience, experience. experience. experience. experience. experience. experience? experienced experienced experiences experiences experiences experiment experiment experiment Experiment experiment experiment experiment Experiment experiment experiment experiment experiment experiment experiment experiment, experiment. experiment. Experiment1) Experimental Experimental experimental experimental experimental experimental experiments experiments experiments. explain explained explained explained explains explanation; explanations. express express express express express express express express expressed expressed expressed expressed Expressed expressed expressed expressed expresses expresses expresses expression expression expression expression expression expression expression expression expression expression expression expression expression expression expression expressions extend extended extended extending extends extends extension extension extension extent extent extent extent extent extent extent, extent. external externally extra-galactic extraneous. eye, F F F F face faced faced fact fact fact fact fact fact fact fact fact fact fact fact fact fact fact fact fact fact fact fact fact fact, fact, fact, fact, fact, fact, factor factor facts facts facts facts facts facts facts, facts. fair fairer fall fall fall fall. falls familiar far far far far far far far far far far far, far, Faraday Faraday-Maxwell far-reaching farther farther farther farther farther farther farther farther farther farther, farther, farther. fashion, fashionundersuitablechoiceofreference-body,i.e.domainsinwhich fast fasten favour favour favour favour favour favour favour favour. favoured feature feel feel feel feel feel feel feeling feeling few Few few Few few few few few few few fictitious field field

field field field field field field field field field Field field field field field field Field field field field field field field field field field field field field field field field field Field field), field, field, field, field, field, field, field, field, field, field. field. field. field. field. field. field. fieldequations fields fields fields fields fields fields fields fields fields fields fields fields fields fields, fields, fields, fields, fields, fields. fields. fifteenth fifth Fig Fig. Fig. Fig. figure fill final finally finally finally Finally, finally, finally, find find find find find find find find find find find find find find find, finds finds finite Finite finite finite finite Finite finite finite finite finite finite finite finite finite. finiteness First First first, first, first, first. first. fit fitted fittingly FitzGerald fix fixed fixes Fizeau Fizeau Fizeau Fizeau Fizeau, Fizeau. Fizeau's flame. flash flash flashes flashes flashes flashes flat flat flat flat Flat flat floor floor floor floor floor floor, floor. flow flowing flying flying foci follow followed followed followed following. follows, follows. follows. foot Footnotes Footnotes Footnotes Footnotes Footnotes Footnotes Footnotes Footnotes Footnotes Footnotes Footnotes Footnotes Footnotes Footnotes Footnotes Footnotes footpath footpath for for for For For For For for for For for for For for for for

for for for for for for for for for for for For For For For for for for for For for for for for for for for for for for for for for for for for for for for for for for for for for for for for for For For for for for for for for for for for for for for for For For For for For For for for for for for for for for for for for for for for for For for for for for For for for for for for for for for For for for for for for for for for for for for for for for for for for for for for for for For for for for for for for for for For for for for for for for for for for for for for for for for For for for For for for for for for for for for for for for for for for for for for for for for for for For for for for for for for for For for for for for for for for for for for for For for for For for for for for for for for for for For for for for For for For, for, force force force force force force force force force force force) force. forces forces. foregoing foregoing foregoing forest foretold form form form form form form form form form form form form form form form form form form form form form form form, form, form. form. form; formal formal formal formal formal formal Formally, former formerly forming forms forms, forms, formula formula formula formula formulate formulate formulate formulated formulated formulated formulated formulated- formulates formulation Formulation Formulation formulation formulation formulation formulation formulation. forth forth forth forth forth forward forward, forwards forwards forwards. found found found found found found found found found found found found found foundation foundation. Foundations Foundations foundations founded founded four four four four four four four four four four four Four-dimensial fourdimensional fourdimensional fourdimensional fourdimensional fourdimensional four-dimensional four-dimensional four-dimensional Four-Dimensional four-dimensional Four-Dimensional four-dimensional four-dimensional Four-Dimensional four-dimensional four-dimensional four-dimensional four-dimensional four-dimensional four-dimensional four-dimensional four-dimensional four-dimensional, fourth fourth fourth fourth fourth fourth fourth frame framework framework framework. framework. frameworks Free free free free free free free free freely freely freely-moving freely-moving frequency frequency frequency frequently frequently frequently frequently, Freundlich Friedman Friedman, Friedman, friend friend from from from from from From from From from From from From From from From from from from from from from from from from from from from from from from from from from from from from from from from from from from from from from from from from from from from from from from from from from from from from from from from from from from from from from from from from from from from from from from from from from from from from from from from from from from from from from from from from from from from from from from from From from from from from from from from from from from from from from from from from from from from from from from from from from from from from from from from from from from From From from from from from from from from from from from from from from from from from from from from from from from from From from from from from from From from from from from from from from from from from from from from from from from from from from from from from From from from from from from from from from from from from from from from from from from from from from from from from from from from from from from from from from from from from from from front front front fulfil fulfilled fulfilled fulfilled full full fully function functions fundamentally furnish further further further further further further further further further further further, Furthermore, furthermore, Furthermore, G G, G. g11, g11, g11, g11du2 g11dx1 g12 g12, g22, g22, g22dv2 g44dx4 gained gained galactic Galfleian Galflei-Newton Galilei Galilei Galilei Galilei Galilei Galilei) Galilei. Galileian

Galileian Galileian Galileian Galileian Galileian Galileian Galileian Galileian Galileian Galileian Galileian Galileian Galileian Galileian Galileian Galileian Galileian Galileian Galileianco-ordinatesystems. Galileianspace Galileiansystemofco-ordinates. Galilei-Newton Galilei-Newton, Galileitransformation. gas gas gas Gauss Gauss Gauss Gauss Gauss Gauss Gauss Gauss Gauss Gauss Gauss Gauss Gauss Gauss, Gaussian Gaussian Gaussian Gaussian Gaussian Gaussian Gaussian Gaussian gave general General General general general General General general General general General general general general general general General general general general general General general general general General general General General General General General General General General General General General General general General general General General General General General General general general General General general general general General general general general general general General general General general General general general General General General general general general general general general general general general General general general general general general General General general General General general general general general general general general general general general general general general, general, general, general, general, generalisation generalisation generalisation generalisation generalisation generalisation generalisation generalised generalised generalised. generality generally generally generally generally generalprincipleofrelativity genesis geometrical

geometrical Geometrical geometrical Geometrical Geometrical geometrical geometrical geometrical geometrical geometrical geometrical geometrical geometrical geometrical geometrical geometrical Geometry Geometry geometry geometry Geometry geometry geometry geometry geometry geometry geometry geometry geometry geometry geometry geometry geometry geometry geometry geometry, geometry, geometry, geometry, geometry, geometry, geometry, geometry. geometry. geometry. geometry. geometry. get get getting give give give give give give give give give given, given. giver gives gives gives giving glance GNU go go go go go go go go, goal goes goes goes goes going gone good good got got got governing governs gradually gradually gradually grant grant granted granted granted grasp grasping grave Gravitation gravitation Gravitation gravitation gravitation gravitation Gravitation gravitation gravitation gravitation, gravitation, gravitation, gravitation. gravitation. gravitation. gravitation. gravitation. gravitation. gravitation.1) gravitational gravitational gravitational gravitational gravitational gravitational gravitational gravitational gravitational gravitational gravitational gravitational Gravitational gravitational Gravitational gravitational gravitational gravitational Gravitational Gravitational gravitational Gravitational Gravitational gravitational

gravitational gravitational gravitational gravitational gravitational gravitational gravitational gravitational gravitational gravitationalmass gravitationial gravititional gravity gravity, grazing great great great great great great great great great great great great great greater greater greater greater greater greatest greatest greatest greatest greatest Grebe grossly ground ground ground ground, grounds grounds group-density grown grows Guided Guided Guided guilty H. H. H. habit habit habit habit had had had had had had had had had had had had had had half half half half hand hand, hand, hand, hand, hand, hand, hand, hand, hand, hand, hand. handling hands hands) hang happen happen happening happy hardly hardly hardly hardly harmony has has has has has has has has has has has has has has has has has has has has has has has has has has has has has has has has has has has has has has has has has has has has has has has has has has has has has has has has has has has has has has has has has has has has has has has has has has has has has has has has has has has has has has has has has has has has has has, hastening have having having he he he he He he he he he he he He he he he he he he he he he He he he he he he he he he he He he he he He he he he he he he he He hears heat heated heating, heavenly heavenly heavenly heavenly heavenly heavens. heaviness height held Helmholtz Helmholtz). help Hence Hence hence Hence Hence hence hence hence hence hence Hence Hence hence Here Here here here here here here here Here here here here here here here here here Here here here here

Here here, here. here. here. hereditary Hereupon Heuristic heuristic high high highest him him him him him him him; himself himself himself himself, himself. his his his his his his his his his his his his his his his his his his his his his Hitherto hitherto hitherto hitherto hitherto hitherto hitherto hitherto hold hold hold hold hold hold hold hold hold hold hold hold hold hold hold hold hold hold hold hold hold hold hold hold hold hold hold, hold, hold. holding holding holding holding holds holds holds holds holds holds holds holds home homogeneous honestly hook hook hope hope hope horn hours hours hovering how how how how how how How how How how how how how How how how how how how how How how Howdoesitcomethatcertainreference-bodies(ortheirstatesofmotion) however however However however However, however, however, however, However, However, however, however, however, however, however, however, However, however, however, however, however, however, however, however, however, however, Hubble Hubble Hubble's Hueristic hundredth hundredths hypothese hypotheses hypotheses hypotheses hypotheses hypotheses hypotheses hypotheses hypotheses hypotheses, hypotheses, hypothesis Hypothesis hypothesis hypothesis hypothesis hypothesis hypothesis hypothesis hypothesis hypothesis hypothesis hypothesis, hypothesis, hypothesis, hypothetical hypothetical hypothetical I, I, I. I. i.e. i.e. i.e. i.e. i.e. i.e. i.e. i.e. i.e. i.e. i.e. i.e. i.e. i.e. i.e. i.e. i.e. i.e. i.e. i.e. i.e. i.e. i.e. i.e. i.e. i.e. I; laws Idea Idea idea idea idea idea idea idea idea idea ideas ideas ideas ideas ideas ideas ideas ideas ideas, ideas, ideas, ideas. ideas. identical identical identical identical identical identical identical identical identical identical identical; identically identically identically. If If if If If If If If If If If If If If If if if If if If if If If if if if if If if If if If if If if If if if If If If if If If If if If if If if if If If If if if if if if if If If If If if If If if If If if If if if if if if if If if if If if if if If if If if If if

If if if If If if If if If If if If If If If if If if if If if If if If if If, If, If, If, If, If, If, If, if, If, If, If, If, ifine, II II II II II II II II II II II II II II II II II II II II II II II II II II II II II II II II II II II II II II II II II II II. II] III III III III III III III III III III III III, III.) lines. illuminated illustration illustration illustration illustration, illustration, imaginary imaginary imaginary imaginary imaginary imaginary. imagine imagine imagine imagine imagine imagine imagine imagine imagine imagine imagine imagine imagine imagine imagine Imagine imagine imagine imagine imagine imagine imagine imagine imagine imagine imagine imagine imagine imagine imagine immaterial immaterial immaterial immediate immediate immediately immediately immense impact impenetrability imperfections implements, implies importance importance importance importance importance importance importance, importance, importance, importance. important important important important important important important important important important important important imposed impossible impossible impossible impossible impossible impossible impossible. impossible. impoverished. improbable. impulse). in In In in in in in In In In In in in In in in in in in In In In In In in in In in In In In In In In In In In In In In In in In In In In in In In in In In in in in in In In in in in in in in in in in In in In in in in in in in in in in in in In in in in In in in in in In in in in in in in in in in in in in in in in in in in in In in in in in in in in in in in in in in in in in in in In in in in in in in In in in in in In in in in in in in in in in in in in in in In in in in in in in in in in in in in in In in in in in in in in in in in in in in in in in In in in in in in in in In in In in in in in in in in in in in in in in in In in in in in in in in in in in in In in in in in in in in in in in in in in in in in in in in in In in in in in in in in in in in in in in in in In in in in in In in in in in in in in In in in in in In In in in in in in in in in in in in in in in in in in In in in in in In in in in in in in in in In in in In in in in in in in in in in in In in in In in in in in In in in in in in in in in in in In in in in in in in in in in in in In in in in in in in in in in in in in in in In in In in in in in in in in in in in in in in in in in in in in in in in in in in in in in in in in in in In in In in in in in in in in In in in In In in in in in in in in In in in in in in in in in In in in in In in in in in In in in in in in in in in in In in In in in in in in in in in in in in in in in in in in In in in in in in in in in in in in in in in in in in in in in in in in in in in in in in in in in in in in in In in in in in in in in in in In in in in in in in in in in In in in in in in in in in in in in in In in in in in in in in in in in in in in in in in in in in in in in in in in in in in in in in in in in in in in in in in in in In in in in in in In in in in in in in in in in in in in in in in In in in In in in in in in in in in in in In in in in In in in in in in in in in in in in in in In in in in in in in in in In in In in in in in in in in in in in in in in in in in inaccuracy inadequate inadequate. incidence incidental incidental inclined inclined inclined include include incomparably incomparably Incompatability incompatibilitiy Incompatibility incompatibility incompatible incomplete incomplete incongruity incorrectness. increase increase increase increased increases increases increases increases increasing increasing increasing increasing indebted indeed indeed indeed, indeed, indefinite indefinitely indefinitely indefinitely independence. independent independent independent independent independent independent independent independent independent independent independent independent independent independent independent independent, independently independently independently independently index indicate indicate indicate indicate indicated indicated indicated indicated indicated indicated indicated indicated indicated, indicated, indicates indicates indicating indirect indirectly. individual individual individual individual individual individual individual individual individual induction. inertia inertia inertia inertia inertia inertia, inertia. inertial inertial inertial inertial inertial inertial Inertial Inertial inertial inertial inertial inertial inertial inertialmass inevitable inexperienced Inferences Inferences infinite infinite infinite infinite infinite infinite infinite infinite

infinite, infinite. infinite. infinite. infinitely infinitely infinitely infinitely infinitely infinitely infiniteness infinity infinity infinity, infinity. influence influence influence influence influence influence influence influence influence influence influence influence influence influenced influenced influenced influenced influences influences influences influences influences influences, information ingenious inhabited inherent inherited initial initial inner innumerable inquire inquire inreality insert insert insert inserting inside inside insight inspace inspace inspace. instance instance instance, instance, instance, instance, instance, instance, instance, instance, instance, instantaneous instantaneous instantaneous instead instead instead Instead instead instead instead instead insufficient insurmountable intellect intellect intellectual intelligible intelligible intended, intensity intensity intensity intention interaction interest interest interested interesting interfere interference interior intermediary intermediary intermediate interpret interpret interpret interpret interpret interpretation interpretation interpretation interpretation interpretation interpretation interpretation interpretation interpretation interpretation, interpreted interpreted interpreted interpreted interpreted. interpreting intersect interval interval intervention into into into into into into into into into into into into into into into into into into into into into into into into into into into into into into into into into into into into into introduce introduce introduce introduce introduce introduce introduce introduce introducing introducing introduction introduction introduction introduction introduction introduction intuition invalid invalid. invalidate invalidates invariable invented inverse inversely investigate investigate investigation investigation investigation investigation, investigations investigations investigations. investigator investigators, invisible. involved involved involved involved, involves involves involves involving involving ions; iron iron, iron, irregular, irregularly is is is is is is is is is is is is is is is is is is is is is is is is is is is is is is is is is is is is is is is is is is is is is is is is is is is is Is is is is is is is is is is is is is is is is is is is is is is is is is is is is is is is is is is is is is is is is is is is is is is is is

is is is is is is is is is is is is is is is is is is is is is is is is is is is
is is is is is is is is is is is is is is is is is is is is is is is is is is is
is is is is is is is is is is is is is is is is is is is is is is is is is is is
is is is is is is is is is is is is is is is is is is is is is is is is is is is
is is is is is is is is is is is is is is is is is is is is is is is is is is is
is is is is is is is is is is is is is is is is is is is is is is is is is is is
is is is is is is is is is is is is is is is is is is is is is is is is is is is
is is is is is is is is is is is is is is is is is is is is is is is is is is is
is is is is is is is is is is is is is is is is is is is is is is is is is is is
is is is is is is is is is is is is is is is is is is is is is is is is is is is
is is is is is is is is is is is is is is is is is is is is is is is is is is is
is is is is is is is is is is is is is is is is is is is is is is is is is is is
Is is is is is is is is is is is is is is is is is is is is is is is is is is is
is is is is is is is is is is is is is is is is is is is is is is is is is is is
is is is is is is is is is is is is is, is, is, is, is, is, isa island island
isolated isolated It It It It It It It it It It It It It It It it It It It It It it It it
it it It It it it it it it it it it it it it it it it it It it it it it it It it it it it it it it
it it it it It it it it it it it It it it it it it it it it it It It it it It it It it It it it
it it It It it it it it It It it it It it it it it it it It it it it it it it it it It It It it
it it it it it it it it it it it it it it it it it it it it it it it it it it It it It it it it it
It it it it it it It it it It it It it it it it It it it It it it it it It It it it it it it it
It it it it it it it it it it it it it it it It it it it it It it it It it It it it it it, it, it,
it, it, it, it. it. it. it. it. it. it. it. it. it. it. it. it. its its its its its its its its
its its its its its its its its its its its its its its its its its its its its its its
its its its its its its its its its its its its its its its its its its its its its its
its its its its its its its its its its its its its its its its its its its its its its
its its itself itself itself itself itself itself itself itself itself itself itself itself
itself itself itself itself itself itself, itself. itself. itself. IV janitor.] jerk jerk
jerk John, joining joining joining Joint judged judged judged judged
judged judged judged judged judged judged judged judged judged
judged judged judged judged judged judged Julius jumps jumps.
juncture juncture juncture just Just just just just just just just Just just

just just just just just justifiable justifiable justifiably justification justification justification justification justified justified justified justified justified justified justified justified, K K K K K K K K K K K K K K K k K K K K K K K K K K K K K K K K K K K K K K K K K K K K' K' K'(t' K) K), K, K, K, K, K, K, K, K, K, K, K, K, K, K, K, K, K, K, K, K, K, K, K, K, K, K, K', K. K. K. K. K. K. K. K. K. K. K. K. K. K. K. K. K. K'. K'. K? K0 K0 K0. K0. K1 K1 K1 K1 K1 K1 K1 K1 K1 K1 K1 K1 K1 K1 K1 K1 K1 K1 K1 K1 K1 K1 K1 K1 K1 K1 K1 K1 K1 K1 K1 K1 K1 K1 K1 K1 K1 K1). K1, K1, K1, K1, K1, K1, K1, K1, K1, K1, K1, K1. K1. K1. K1. K1. K1. K1. K1. K1. K1.1) K2, key, kilometres kind kind kind kind kind kind kind kind kind kind kind kind kind kind kind kind kind). kind). kind, kind. kind. kinds kinetic kinetic kinetic km./sec. knew know know know know know know know know know knowledge knowledge knowledge knowledge, knowledge, knowledge, known known known known known known known known known known known known known known, known, known. known. known. known/identifiable knows, knows, L. laid laid laid laid laid laid laid, lake. land, large large large large large large large large large large large large large large large larger larger largest last last last last last last last later later later later later later later. later. later. later. later. laterally latter, latter. lattice law law law law Law law law law law law law law law law law law law law law law law law law law law law law law law law law law law law law law law law law law Law law law law law law law law law law law law law law law law law law law law law law law law law law law law law law law law law law law law law law law law law law law law law law law law law law law law, law, law, law, law, law, law. law. law. law. law. law-of-field laws laws laws laws laws laws laws laws laws laws laws laws laws laws laws laws laws laws laws laws laws laws laws laws laws laws laws laws laws laws laws laws laws laws laws laws laws laws laws laws laws laws laws laws laws laws laws laws laws laws, laws, laws, laws, laws. laws. lawsofnature

Lawson lay lays lead lead lead, leading leads leads leads leads leads leads leads learn learn learn learn least least least least least least least least least least. leave leave leave led led led led led led led led led led led left left left left-hand left-hand legitimately legs length length length length length length length length length length length length length length length length length length, length, length, length, length. lengths lengths lengths lengths lengths lengths lengths, lengths. less less less less less less less less less less less less less less less. Let Let Let Let Let Let Let Let Let Let let Let let Let Let Let Let Let Let let let let let let Let Let Let Let Leverrier, lib. License. lid lid lid, lie lie lie lie lie lies lies lies lies lies lies lies. life. light light light light light light Light light light light light light light light light light light light light Light light light light light light light light Light light Light light). light, light, light, light, light, light, light, light. light. light. light. light. light; Lightning lightning lightning lightning lightning lightning lightning lightning lightning lightning lightning lightning light-signal light-signal light-signal light-signal, light-stimulus like like like like like like like like likely likely likely likewise likewise likewise likewise likewise likewise limit limitation limitation. limitations limited, limiting limiting limiting limiting limiting limits limits. line line line line line line line line line line line line line line line line line line line line line line, line, line. line. line. line. line. line. line. line. linear lines lines lines lines lines lines Lines lines lines lines lines lines lines lines lines lines lines lines lines lines lines lines lines. lineshift linesofforce liquid liquid liquid liquid liquid, liquid. liquid. little little little little little little little little little little little little little little little little litttle live live lives living living living load local local localised localised localised locate locating location lodged lofty logical logical logical logical logical logically logically long long long long long long long long long

long long long long. longer longer longer longer longer longer longer longer longer longer longer. looked Lorentztransformation. loses love Ltd lucidity lucidity luminous lying M M M m M M m m M, m, m. M1 M1 M1 Mach made made made made made made made made made made made made, magnet magnet magnet magnet. magnetic magnetic magnetic magnetic magnificent magnitude magnitude magnitude magnitude magnitude magnitude magnitude magnitude magnitude magnitude magnitude, magnitudes magnitudes magnitudes magnitudes magnitudes magnitudes magnitudes magnitudes magnitudes magnitudes magnitudes main main main main maintain maintain maintain maintain maintain maintained maintained maintained, maintained. maintains maintenance, major major make make make make make make make make make make make make make make make makes makes making making making making making making making making man man man man man man man man man man man man man man man man man man man man man man manifest manifested manifests manifests manipulations manner, manner, manner, manner, manner, manner. manner. manner. manner. manner. manner. manner. manner. manner. many many many many many many many marble marble marble marble marble marble marble marble marble marble marble marble marble marble mark mark marked marked marked marked marking marks Mass mass Mass mass mass mass mass mass mass mass mass mass mass mass mass Mass mass mass mass mass mass mass mass mass mass mass) mass) mass, mass. mass. mass. masses masses masses masses

masses masses masses masses masses, material material material Material material material material material material material material material material material material material material material material) mathematical mathematical mathematical mathematical mathematical mathematical mathematical mathematically Mathematically, mathematician Mathematicians mathematicians mathematics, matriculation matter, matter. matter. matter. matters mature maximum maximum, maximum, Maxwell Maxwell Maxwell Maxwell-Lorentz Maxwell-Lorentz Maxwell-Lorentz Maxwell-Lorentz Maxwell-Lorentz Maxwell-Lorentz Maxwell-Lorentz, may may may may may may may may may may may may may may may may may may may may may may may May may may may may may may may may may may may may may May, May, mc2 mc2 mc2, me me me me me me. Mean mean mean mean mean mean mean mean mean mean meaning meaning Meaning meaning Meaning meaning meaning meaning meaning meaning meaning meaning, meaning. meaning. meaningless means. meant measaring-rod measurable measure measure measure measure measure measure measure. measure. measured measured measured measured measured measured measured measured measured measured measured measured measurement measurement measurement measurement measurement measurement measurement. measurements measurements measurements measurements measurements) measurements. measurements. measurements. measurements. measurements. measures measures measures measuring measuring measuring-rod measuring-rod measuring-rod measuring-rod measuring-rod measuring-rod measuring-rod) measuring-rod, measuringrod. measuring-rod. measuringrods Measuring-Rods measuring-rods measuring-rods Measuring-Rods measuring-rods Measuring-Rods Measuring-Rods measuring-rods measuring-rods measuring-rods measuring-rods measuring-rods measuringrods, measuring-rods, measuring-rods, measuring-rods, measuring-rods, measuring-rods, measuring-rods, measuring-rods. measuring-rods. mechanical mechanical mechanical mechanical mechanical mechanical Mechanics Mechanics mechanics mechanics mechanics mechanics Mechanics mechanics mechanics mechanics mechanics mechanics Mechanics mechanics mechanics mechanics mechanics mechanics mechanics Mechanics mechanics mechanics mechanics Mechanics mechanics mechanics mechanics- mechanics), mechanics, mechanics, mechanics, mechanics, mechanics, mechanics, mechanics, mechanics, mechanics. mechanics. mechanics; mechanics; medium) medium. meet meet meet meet mention mention mention mentioned mentioned mentioned mentioned mentioned mentioned mentioned mentioned mentioned mentioned, mentioned, Mercury Mercury Mercury Mercury Mercury Mercury, Mercury, Mercury, Mercury, merely merits meteorologist method method method method method method method method method method method method method. methods methods methods Methuen metre. metre-rod metre-rod metre-rod metre-rod metre-rod metrics Michelson Michelson Michelson middle middle middle midpoint mid-point mid-point might might might might might might might might might milky millimetre millionths minimum minimum minimum. Minkowski Minkowski Minkowski, Minkowski, Minkowski. Minkowski's Minkowski's Minkowski's Minkowski's Minkowski's mirror mirror mirrors mirrors mirrors mirrors, misconception misdeed mistaken mode mode mode mode mode mode Modern modification modification modification modification modification modification modified modified modify moduate mollusc mollusc mollusc mollusc mollusc. molluscs moment moment moment moment. momentary months more more more more more more more more more more more more more more more more more more more more more more More more more

more more more more more more more more more more more more more more more more more more more more more more, Moreover, Moreover, Moreover, Moreover, Moreover, moreover, Morley Morley most most most most most most most most most most most most most most most most most most most most motion motion motion motion motion motion motion motion motion motion motion motion Motion motion motion motion motion motion motion motion motion Motion motion Motion motion) motion, motion, motion, motion, motion, motion, motion, motion, motion, motion, motion, motion. motion. motion. motion. motion. motion. motion. motion. motion. motion. motion. motion. motion. motion. motion. motion. motion. motion. motion. motionless motionrelativetoapracticallyrigidbodyofreference. motions motions motions motions motions motions motions, move move move move move move move move move movement movement movement movement movement moves moves moves moves moves. moving, much much much much much much multi-dimensional, must must must must must must must must must must must must must must must must must must must must must must must must must must must must must must must must must must must must must must must must must must must must must must must must must must must must must must must must must must must must must must must must must must must must must must must must must must must must, mutual mutually My my my my my Mybodyof myself myself mysterious name

Namely, Namely, namely, namely, namely, names) naturally naturally naturally naturally nature), nature), nature, nature, nature, nature, nature. nature. nature. nature. nature. nature. nature; Naturwissenschaften, near near nearest nearly nebulae nebulae. necessarily necessarily necessarily necessarily necessarily necessarily necessarily necessarily necessarily necessarily necessary necessary necessary necessary necessary necessary necessary necessary necessity necessity necessity need need need need need need need needs negative negative negative negative negative negative negative. negative. negatively negatively, negligibly neighbour. neighbourhood neighbourhood neighbourhood neighbourhood neighbouring neighbouring neighbouring neighbouring neighbouring neighbouring neither neither neither neither neither neither neither neutralised never never never never never Nevertheless nevertheless nevertheless nevertheless nevertheless Nevertheless, nevertheless, Nevertheless, New New new new new new new new new new new new. Newcomb Newton Newton Newton Newton Newton, Newton, Newton. Newton. Newtonian Newtonian Newtonian Newtonian Newtonian Newton-Kepler Newton's Newton's Newton's Newton's Newton's Newton's Newton's Newton's Newton's Newton's Newton's Newton's next next next next next next.) nil. no no no no no no no no no no no no no no no no no no no no no no no no no no no no no no no no no no no no no no no no no no no no no No no no no no no no no No. noble nobody non-non-equivalence Non-Euclidean non-Euclidean non-Euclidean non-Euclidean non-Euclidean nonmathematician non-mathematician non-rigid non-rigid non-rigid non-rotary nonrotating non-uniform non-uniform non-uniformity non-uniformly non-uniformly non-uniformly nor nor nor nor nor

nor nor nor nor nor nor Not not not not not not not not not not not not not not not not not not not not not not not not not not not not not not not not not not not not not not not not not not not not not not not not not not not not not not not Not not not not not not not not not not not not not not not not not not not not not not not not not not not not not not not not not not not not not not not not not not not not not not not not not not not not not not not Not not not not not not not not not not not not not not not not not not not not not not not not not not not not not not not not not not not not not not not not not not not not not not not not not not not, not. not. not. notable Note note note Note, noted Notes Notes Notes nothing nothing nothing nothing nothing nothing nothing nothing nothing nothing nothing notice notice notice notice notice. notices notion notion Now now Now now Now Now Now now now now now now now now now now now now now Now now now now now now now now now Now now now Now now Now now Now now Now now Now Now, now, now, nowhere number,2) number. number. numbering numbers numbers numbers numbers numbers numbers numbers numbers numbers numbers, numbers, numbers, numbers. numbers. numerical numerical numerical numerically numerically numerous O object object object object object, object; objection objection objection objection objection objective objects objects objects objects obscure observa- observation observation observation observation observation observation observation observation observation observation observation observation, observation. observation. observation. observation. observations observations observations observations observations observations, observations. observe observe observe observe observed observed observed observed observed observed observed observed observed observer

observer. observers Observers observes obtaill obtain, obtainable obtainable obtained. obvious obvious obvious obvious Obviously Obviously obviously Obviously occult. occupant occupant occupied occupies occur occur occur, occur. occurred occurred occurrence occurrence occurs, ocean of of of of of of of of of of Of of of of of of Of of of of of of of of of of of Of of Of of

of of of of of of of of of of of of of of of of of of of of of of of of of
of of of of of of of of of of of of of of of of of of of of of of of of of
of of of of of of of of of of of of of of of of of of of of of of of of of
of of of of of of of of of of of of of of of of of of of of of of of of of
of of of of of of of of of of of of of of of of of of of of of of of of of
of of of of of of of of of of of Of of of of of of of of of of of of of of
of of of of of of of of of of of of of of of of of of of of of of of of of
of of of of of of of of of of of of of of of of of of of of of of of of of
of of of of of of of of of of of of of of of of of of of of of of of of of
of of of of of of of of of of of of of of of of of of of of of of of of of
of of of of of of of of of of of of of of of of of of of of of of of of of
of of of of of of of of of of of of of of of of of of of of of of of of of
of of of of of of of of of of of of of of of of of of of of of of of of of
of of of of of of of of of of of of of of of of of of of of of of of of of
of of of of of of of of of of of of of of of of of of of of of of of of of
of of of of of of of of of of of of of of of of of of of of of of of of of
of of of of of of of of of of of of of of of of of of of of of of of of of
of of of of of of of of of of of of of of of of of of of of of of of of of
of of of of of of of of of of of of of of of of of of of of of of of of of
of of of of of of of of of of of of of of of of of of of of of of of of of
of of of of of of of of of of of of of of of of of of of of of of of of of
of of of of of of of of of of of of of of of of of of of of of of of of of
of of of of of of of of of of of of of of of of of of of of of of of of of
of of of of of of of of of of of of of of of of of of of of of of of of of
of of of of of of of of of of of of of of of of of of of of of of of of of
of of of of of of of of of of of of of of of of of of of of of of of of of
of of of of of of of of of of of of of of of of of of of of of of of of of
of of of of of of of of of of of of of of of of of of of of of of of of of
of of of of of of of of of of of of of of of of of of of of of of of of of
of of of of of of of of of of of of of of of of of of of of of of of of of
of of of of of of of of of of of Of of of of of of of of of of of of of of
of of of of of of of of of of of of of of of of of of of of of of of of of

of of of of of of of of of of of of of of of of of of of of of of of of of
of of of of of of of of of of of of of of of of of of of of of of of of of
of of of of of of of of of of of of of of of of of of of of of of of of of
of of of of of of of of of of of of of of of of of of of of of of of of of
of of of of of of of of of of of of of of of of of of of of of of of of of
of of of of of of of of of of of of of of of of of of of of of of of of of
of of of of of of of of of of of of of of of of of of of of of of of of of
of of of of of of of of of of of of of of of of of of of of of of of of of
of of of of of of of of of of of of of of of of of of of of of of of of of
of of of of of of of of of of of of of of of of of of of of of of of of of
of of of of of of of of of of of of of of of of of of of of of of of of of
of of of of of of of of of of of of of of of of of of of of of of of of of
of of of of of of of of of of of of of of of of of of of of of of of of of
of of of of of of of of of of of of of of of of of of of of of of of of of
of of of of of of of of of of of of of of of of of of of of of of of of of
of of of of of of of of of of of of of of of of of of of of of of of of of
of of of of of of of of of of of of of of of of of of of of of of of of of
of of of of of of of of of of of of of of of of of of of of of of of of of
of of of of of of of of of of of of of of of of of of of of of of of of of
of of of of of of of of of of of of of of of of of of of of of of of of of
of of of of of of of of of of of of of of of of of of of of of of of of of
of of of of of of of of of of of of of of of of of of of of of of of of of
of of of of of of of of of of of of of of of of of of of of of of of of of
of of of of of of of of of of of of of of of of of of of of of of of of of
of of of of of of of of of of of of of of of of of of of of of of of of of
of of of of of of of of of of of of of of of of of of of of of of of of of
of of of of of of of of of of of of of of of of of of of of of of of of of
of of of of of of of of of of of of of of of of of of of of of of of of of
of of of of of off off off off off off off offer
ofK1fromK;thismeansthatwehavetoinsertaparticularvalueoft(timeof often
o f t e n o f t e n o f t h e c l o c k) r e l a t i v e t o K
ofthesameeventswithrespecttoK.ButthediscoveryofMinkowski, old old older

old-time On On on On on On On On on on on on on On On on on on on on on on on on on on on on on on on on on on on on on on on on on on on on on on on on on on on on on on on on on on on on on on on on on on on on on on on on On on on on on on on on on on on on on on on on on on on on on on on on on on on on on on on on on On on on on on on on on on on on on on on on on on On on on on on on on on on on on on on on on On On on on on on on on on on on on on on on on on on on on on on on on on on on on on on On on on on on on on on on on on on on On on on on on on on On on On on on on on on on on on on on on on on on once Once once one one one one one one one one One one one one one one one one one one one one one one one one one one one one one one one one one one one one one one one one one one one one one one one one one one one one one one one one one one one one one one one one one one one, one, one, one, one, one, one, one, one, one. one. one. one. ones, ones. only Only only only only only only only only only only only only only only only only only only only only only only only only only only only only only only only only only only only only only only only only only only only only only only only only only only only only only only only only only only only only only only only only only only only only only only only only only only. only. open operates operating operation operations operations operative opinion opinion opinion opinion opponents opposed opposed opposes opposite opposition optical optical optics optics. or or or or or or or or or or or or or or or or or or or or or or or or or or or or or or or or or or or or Or or or or or or or or or or or or or or or or or or or or or or or or or or, or, or, or, or, or, or, or, oras orbit orbit orbit orbit orbit orbit orbit orbit orbital orbital orbital orbital orbital order ordinary ordinates ordinates ordinates), ore organpipe orientation orientation orientation orientation. origin origin origin origin origin origin

origin origin, original original original original original original original original originally originated. ot other). other, other, other, other, other, other, other, other, other, other, other. other. other. other. other. other. other. other. other. other. other. other. other. others others others otherwise otherwise ought Ought ought ought ought ought ought ought ought ought ought ought ought ought ought our Our our our our our our our our our our our our our our our our our our our our our our Our our our our our our our our our our our our our our our our our our our our our our our our our our our our our our our our our our our our our our our our our our our our our our our our our our our our Our Our our Our our our our our our our our our our our our our our our our our our ours, ours, ourselves ourselves ourselves ourselves ourselves ourselves out out out out out out out out out out out out out out out out out out out out out out, out. outer out-of-the-way outset outset, outside outside outwards outwards outwards outwards outwards. over over over over over over over over over over over over over over over, overcome. overlapping. overthrown overthrown owing owing owing owing owing owing Owing owing own own own own own own P P P P p P p. p. p. p0 p0 p0 p0R. p0V. P1 P1 P1, P1, pages pages pages, pains pair pan pan pan, pans pans. paper parabola. parabola? parabolic paragraphs. parallel parallel parallel pardonable. part Part

part part Part part part part part part part part part part part part part part part part part part part part part Part part part) part, part. part. particle particles particles particles particles particles particular, particularly particularly particularly parts parts parts parts, pass pass pass pass pass. passed passes passing passing passing passing passing passing past path path path pathcurve patience patience paying pedantic). pedestrian People per per per per per per per per perceive perceives perceptible perceptible perfectly perfectly perfectly perfectly perfectly perforce perform performed performed performed performed performs Perhaps perhaps perhaps perhaps perhaps perhaps perhaps perhelion perihelial Perihelion perihelion perihelion perihelion) perihelionóclosest period period period periodic periphery, permanent permanently permanently permanently permanently permanently permanently permanently permissible Permission permission permit permits permits pernumently perpendicular perpendicular perpendicular perpendicular perpendicularly perpendicularly perpendiculars perpendiculars perpendiculars perpetually perplexing person person phenomena phenomena phenomena phenomena phenomena phenomena phenomena phenomena phenomena) phenomena, phenomena, phenomena, phenomena, phenomena. phenomena. phenomena. phenomenon philosophical photograph photograph photograph, photographed photographic photographs photographs photographs photographs photographs, Physical physical physical physical physical Physical physically physically physically physically physically physicist physicist physicist physicist physicist physicist), physicists physicists physicists

physicists physicists, physicists, physicists. physics physics physics physics physics Physics physics Physics physics physics physics physics physics physics, physics, physics. physics. physics. pick picture piece piece piece piece piece piece piece pipe pivot Place place, place, place, place, place, place, place. placed placed placed placed placed placed placed places places places places places places places places places plan plan plane plane plane plane plane plane plane plane plane plane plane plane plane plane plane, plane, plane, plane, plane, plane. plane. plane. planes planes planes, planes. planet planet planet planet planet planet planet planet planet planet planet planet. planet. planet. planets planets Planets planets planets, planets, planet-year, plausibility plausible, play played played played plays plays plays plays plays plays plays plays plays pleased plunged PoincarÈ, point, point, point, point, point, point. point. point. point.) pointed pointed pointers pointers pointers point-event pointing point-mass; points) points. points. points. points; poised pole pole pole pole pole pole, ponder popular portion portion portrayed position position position position position position position position position position position position position position position position

position position, position, position. position. position. position. positions positions positions positions positions positions positions positions positions positions positions positions positive positive positive possess possess possess possessed possessed possesses possesses possessing possessing possessing possessing possession possibilities Possibility Possibility possibility possibility possibility possibility possible, possible. possible. possible. possibly postitlate Postulate postulate postulate postulate postulate postulate postulate postulate postulate postulates Postule potential potential potential potential potential, PotsdamerPlatz,Berlin power power powerful powerful powerful powerful powerless. pp. practically practically practically practically practically practically practice practice, practice, practice, practice, practice. practice. preceding preceding preceding preceding preceding precept precisely, precision precision precision. predict predicted predicted predictions Preface Preface preference preference Preference? preferred prejudices premises, prepare pre-relativity preseat presence present, present, present, present, present. presentation presentation presentation. presents presents presents preserve pressure presumes pretence prevailing prevailing prevailing prevails). previous previous previous previous previous previous previous previous previous previous previously previously prime prime primitive Principe principle principle principle principle principle principle Principle Principle Principle Principle principle principle principle Principle Principle Principle principle Principle principle principle principle principle principle Principle principle principle

principle principle principle Principle principle principle principle principle principle principle principle principle principle principle Principle principle principle principle principle Principle principle). principle, principle, principle. principles principles principles principles, priori Priori priori priori; priority pro. probability, probable, probable. problem problem Problem Problem Problem problem problem problem problem problem problem problem problem, problem, problems proceed proceed proceed proceed proceed proceed proceed proceed proceed proceed proceeding proceeding proceeding proceeding process process process process process process process process Process process process process process process process) process, process, process, processes processes processes, processes, produce produced produced produced produced produced produced produced produced. produces produces produces produces profound projected prominence Prominent pronounce pronounced Proof propagated propagated propagated propagated propagation propagation propagation Propagation propagation propagation propagation propagation propagation propagation propagation propagation propagation Propagation propagation propagation propagation propagation propagation propagation propagation propagation propagation propagation propagation properties properties properties properties properties properties properties, properties; property property property property property property, proportional proportional proportional proportional proportional proportional proportional proportionally proposition proposition proposition proposition propositions propositions propositions Propositions propositions propositions propositions Propositions propositions propositions propositions propositions propositions propositions propositions, proud proved proved proven. proves provided provided provided provided provided provided provided province proximity psychological publication Published Publisher publisher. pulled pulling purchase pure Pure purely purely purely purely

purely purely purely purely purponse. purpose purpose purpose purpose purpose, purpose. purposely purposely pursuance pursue pursuit put puts puzzled quadrilateral quadrilateral quality quantitatively. quantity quasi-Euclidean quasi-Euclidean quasi-Euclidean. quasi-spherical. question, question. question. question. question. questions quickly quickly quickly quickly quickly, quite quite quite quite quite quite quite quite quite quite quite quite quite quite quite quite quite quite quite quotient R r r R r R r r r' r, r, r, R.W.L. radial radial radially radiate radiation radioactive radius radius radius radius radius radius radius radius radius radius radius radius radius radius radius. radius. rails rails rails rails rails, railway-carriage railwayembankment. raise raised random range range range. rapid rapid rapidly rate rate rate rate rate rate, rate. rates rates rather rather rather rather rather Rather rather rather rather ratio ratio ratio ratio ratio raven raven raven ray ray ray ray ray ray ray ray ray ray ray ray ray ray ray ray ray) rays rays rays rays rays rays rays rays rays rays rays rays reach reach reach reach reached reached reached reached reached, reaches reaches reaching reaching reaching reaction read reader reader reader reader reader reader reader reader reader reader reader reader. reader. reader. readers readers readily readily reading readings ready real real real real real real real real real real realily realisation realisation realise realised realised, reality reality reality reality reality reality reality reality reality reality reality reality reality, reality. reality. reality. reality. realized really really Realtivity Realtivity reason reason reason reason reason reason reason reason reason reason reason reason reason reason reason reason. reason. reasonable reasons reasons receive recent recent recent recognise

recognise recognised recognised recognised recognises, recognition recognition recognition recognsed reconciled recorded rectangular rectangular rectangular rectilinear rectilinear rectilinear rectilinear rectilinearly red red Red red red reduced reduced reduced. refer refer refer refer refer refer refer refer refer reference reference reference reference reference reference reference reference reference reference Reference reference reference Reference reference Reference reference reference reference reference reference reference reference reference reference reference reference reference reference) reference, reference, reference, reference, reference, reference. reference. reference. reference. reference. reference. reference. reference. reference. reference. reference. reference. reference-bodies reference-bodies reference-bodies reference-bodies reference-bodies reference-bodies reference-bodies reference-bodies reference-bodies, reference-bodies, reference-bodies, reference-bodies. reference-bodies. referencebody referencebody referencebody referencebody reference-body) reference-body). referencebody, reference-body, reference-body, reference-body, reference-body, reference-body, referencebody. reference-body. reference-body. reference-mollusc, Referred referred referred referred referred referred, referred, referred.

refers refers, refers; refinement refinement reflecting reflection refraction refrain refrained refrangible regarded Regarded regarded regarded regarded regarded regarded regarded regarded regarded regarded regarded regarded regarded, regarding regardless regards regards regards regards regards regards regards regards region region regions registration regularly reject relation relation relation relation relation relation relation relation relation relation relation relations relations relations relations relations relations relationship relationship relationship, relationships relative Relative relative Relative relative relative relative relative relative relative relative relative relative relative relative relative relative relative relative relative relative relative relative Relative relative relative relative relative relative relative relative relative relative relative relative relative relatively relatively relatively relatively relatively relatively relatively relatively relatively relatively relatively relatively relatively relatively relativetoK1)wereattributedthemore relativity Relativity Relativity relativity relativity relativity Relativity relativity Relativity relativity Relativity Relativity Relativity Relativity Relativity relativity relativity Relativity relativity relativity relativity Relativity relativity Relativity Relativity Relativity relativity relativity relativity Relativity Relativity relativity Relativity Relativity Relativity Relativity Relativity Relativity relativity relativity Relativity relativity relativity Relativity relativity Relativity Relativity Relativity relativity

Relativity Relativity relativity relativity relativity relativity relativity relativity relativity relativity relativity relativity Relativity relativity Relativity Relativity Relativity Relativity Relativity Relativity Relativity Relativity Relativity Relativity Relativity relativity Relativity relativity relativity relativity relativity Relativity relativity relativity relativity relativity relativity relativity relativity Relativity relativity relativity relativity relativity Relativity relativity Relativity Relativity relativity Relativity relativity relativity relativity relativity relativity relativity relativity relativity Relativity Relativity relativity) relativity) relativity, relativity. relatvity. releases reliable reluctance Relying remain remain remain remain remain remain remained remained remaining remaining remaining remains remark remarkable remarked remarks remedy remember remove removed removed removed removed removed removed. removing rendered renders renders repeat repeated repeated repeatedly repeating repel replace replace replace replace replace replace replaced replaced replaced replaced replacement replaces represent represent represent represent represent representation represented represented represented represented represented represented represented represented represented. represents represents represents re-printing repulsions, request require require require require require require require require require require require required required required required required required required required required required required required required required required, required, requirement requirement requires requires requires requires requires requires requires requiring rernark rescued resemblance resembling resistance, resolve resolves respective Respects Respects respects rest rest rest rest rest rest rest rest rest rest rest rest rest rest rest rest rest rest rest rest rest rest rest rest rest) rest). rest, rest, rest, rest, rest. rest. rest. rest. rest. restricted restricted Restricted restricted restrictions rests results result, result, result, result. result. result. result. resulted resulting resulting resulting resulting resulting results results

results Results results results Results results results results results results results results results results results results results results results retain retain retaining retarded retention return return return, Returning revealed revealed revert revolution revolution revolution revolution revolving rid riding Riemann. Riemman right right right right right right, righthand rightly rigidly rigidly rigidly rigidly rigidly ripe rippled rise robbed Robert rod rod rod rod rod rod rod rod rod rod rod) rod, rod, rod, rod. rods rods rods rods rods rods rods rods rods rods rods rods rods rods rods rods rods rods, rods, rods, rods, rods, rods, rods. rods. rods. role role role, room room room room. root rope rope rope rope rope rope rope rope rope, rope. rope. rotary rotate rotate rotates rotates rotates Rotating rotating rotating rotating rotating rotating Rotating rotating rotation rotation rotation rotation rotation rotation, rotation. rough round round round round round round round round Royal Royal Royal Royal rule rules rules rules run run Russian S S) sacred said said, said, same same same same same same same same same same same same same same same same same same same same same same same same same same same same same same same same same same same same same same same same same same same same same same same same same same same same same same same same same same same same same same same same same same same same same same same same same same same same same same same same same same same. same. samply satisfactorily satisfactory satisfactory satisfactory satisfactory satisfactory. satisfactory. satisficd satisfied satisfied satisfied satisfied satisfied satisfied satisfied satisfied satisfied satisfied, satisfied. satisfies satisfies satisfy satisfy satisfy satisfy satisfy satisfy satisfy satisfy satisfy satisfy satisfying save saw say say say say say say say say say say say say say, saying saying says scarcely scattered scene scene scene scenes school school. schooldays Schwarzschild science science science science science. scientific

scientific scrupulously search second second second second second second second second second second second second second second second second second second second, second, second, second, second. seconds seconds seconds seconds seconds seconds seconds seconds seconds, seconds-clock Section Section Section section Section Section Section Section Section section Section Section section Section Section Section Section Section Section Section section Section Section Section Section Section section Section section Section Section Section Section Section Section Section Section Section Section Section Section Section Section Section Section Section section), section, section, section. section. section. Sections Sections sections see see see see see see see see see see see see see see see see see see see see see seeing seek Seeliger Seeliger. seem seems seems seems seen seen seen seen seen seen seen seen seen seen seen seen seen seized selected selection selfcontained self-evident). self-evident, self-evident. semi-axis sends sense) sense) sense) sense) Sense) sense). sense, sense. sensible sensible sensibly sent sent sent sent separate separated separated separated sequence series series, serious serious serve serve serve serves serves set set set set set set set sets sets settings settled, several several several shalll shape. short short short short short, short, shortened shortened, shortening shortening shorter shorter shortness should Should show show show show show show show show show show show. showed showed, shown shown shown shown shown shown shown shows shows shows shows shows shows shows, shows, shuddering shun side side side side, side. sides sides sight. sign signal significance significance significance significance, significance, signification signify similar similar similar similar similar similar similar similar similarity similarly Similarly, Similarly, Similarly, Simple simple Simple simple simple simple simple simple simple simple simple simple simple simple simple simple simple simple simple simple simple. simpler simplest simplest simplicity simplicity, simplified simply simply simply simply simply simply simply simply Simulatneity simultaneity Simultaneity simultaneity simultaneity simultaneity simultaneity). simultaneity. simultaneity. simultaneity; simultaneous simultaneous simultaneous simultaneous simultaneous simultaneous simultaneous simultaneous simultaneous simultaneous simultaneous. simultaneously simultaneously simultaneously simultaneously simultaneously, simultaneously, simultaneously. simultaneously. Since Since Since Since Since since since since since since since since since since since Since Since since since since since since since since since since since since, single single single singular, sins sins. Sirius, Sitter sitting sitting sitting situated situated situated situated situated situated situated situated situated situated situated situated situated. situated. situation situation size size. size-relations sky sky, slab slab slab slab slab slab slab slab slab), slab, slab, slab, slab, slab. slab. slight slightest slightest slightest slightly slightly slightly slightly slovenliness slower slowly slowly slowly slurs small, smaller smaller smaller smaller smallness smallness smallness. smile smoothly, snapshot snapshot snapshot snapshots So so so so so so so so so so so so so so So so so so so so so so so so so so so so so so so so so so so so so so so, so. Sobral so-called so-called societies Societies, Society Society solar solar solar solar solar sole sole solely solid Solution Solution solution solution solution solution

solution solution solution. solution. solved solved some some some some some some some some some some some some some something something something something something something something something something something something something something something somewhat somewhat somewhat somewhat somewhat somewhat somewhat soon soon sought Source source space Space Space space Space Space space space space space space space Space space Space Space space Space Space space Space Space space space space space space space space space Space space- space) space) space) space). space, space, space, space, space, space, space, space, space, space, space, space, space. space. space. space. space. space. space. space. space. space. space. 1) space.2) space? space-data space-distance space-distribution space-expanse space-interval space-measurements space-point, spaces spacetime space-time space-time Space-Time Space-Time space-time Space-Time Space-Time space-time space-time space-time space-time space-time space-time space-time space-time space-time space-time space-time space-time space-time space-time space-time space-time space-time space-time spacious spared spatial spatially speak speak speak speak speak speak speak speakers speaking speaking, special Special Special special special Special Special Special Special special Special special Special Special Special Special Special Special Special Special Special Special Special Special special special Special Special Special Special Special Special Special Special Special Special Special Special Special Special Special Special Special Special special Special special Special special special special special special special

special specially specially speciallymarkedout) species specific specification specification specification specification specification specification specification specification specification. specifications specify spectral spectral spectral Spectral spectral spectral spectral spectral spectral spectral spectrum spectrum speculations speculations Speical Speical sphere sphere sphere sphere sphere sphere sphere, sphere. sphere-beings sphere-universe spherical spherical spherical spherical spherical spherical spherical spherical spherical spherical spherical spherical spherical spherical spherical spherical spherical spherical spherical, spherical, spherical-surface spirit spite spite spread Springer, square square square square square square square square square square square square), Square, Square, Square, square-root squares squares squares squares squares squares squares. squares. St. stage stage stage. stages, staircase stand stand stand standard standard standard standard standard standing standing Standing standpoint standpoint standpoint standpoint stands star star star star star star star, stars, stars, stars, stars, stars, stars. stars. start start start start started starting starting starting starting Starting starts stated stated stated stated stated Stated stated statement statement statement statement statement statement statement statement statement statement statement statement statement statement statement statement statement statement, statement, statements statements statements statements statements statements, statements. states states static stationary statistical steam steam steam, stellar stellar stellar step step step step-motherly still still still still still still still still still still still still still still still stipulation stipulation stone

stone stone stone stone stone stone stone stone straightline, straightlines straightlines, strange strech stretch strict strictly strictly Strictly strictly strike strike strings strings strives strives strokes strokes strokes strokes strongly struck structure Structure structure Structure Structure Structure structure structure structure structure structure, structure, struggle studied. study study study styled Subject subject subject subject. subject. subsequent substances substitute substitute substituting substitutions subtle subtle subtracting) succeeded success success success success. successful. successfully successive such Such such such such such such Such such such such such such such such such such such such such such such such such such such such such such such such such such such such such such such such such such such Such such such such such such such such such such such such such such such such such such such such such such such such such such such such such such such, suffer suffer suffering suffering suffice suffice sufficient sufficient sufficient sufficient sufficient sufficiently sufficiently sufficiently sufficiently sufficiently sufficiently suggest suggest suggested suggested suggestion suggestion suggestion, suggestive suggests suggests suitable suitable suitably suitably sum sum sum sun sun sun sun sun sun sun sun sun sun sun sun sun sun sun sun sun) sun, sun, sun, sun, sun, sun, sun, sun,1) sun. sun. sun. sun. Sun. sun. sun. sun-planet sun-planet sun-planet sun-planet sun-radii sun's sunóto supplement supplemented supplemented supplemented supplemented supplemented supplementing supplied supplied supplies supplies supplies supplies supplies supplies supplies supply supply support support supported Suppose Suppose suppose suppose suppose suppose suppose suppose suppose suppose suppose suppose, supposed supposed supposed Supposing supposing supposition supposse sure sure surely surface surface surface surface surface surface surface surface surface surface surface surface surface

surface surface, surface, surface. surface. surface. surface. surface. surface. surface. surfaces surfaces surfaces surfaces surfaces, surfaces. surmount surmount surprised surprised. surprises surprising, surrounding surrounding suspended suspended swarm symbol symmetry. system system system system system system system system system system System system system system system system System System system system system system system System system) system) system). system). system); system, system, system, system, system, system. system. system. system. systematic systematic systematically systematically systemofco-ordinates, systems systems systems systems systems systems systems systems systems systems systems systems systems systems systems, systems, systems, systems. t t t t t T t t t t t t T T t t t t t' t) t, t, t, t, t, t, t, t, t, t, t, t', t', t. t. t. t'. t1 t1 t1 T1 t1 t1 T1 t1, t1, t1, t1. t1=0 t1=I Table table table table table table table table, table. table. table. table. table. table. tacit tacitly tacitly tailor take take take take take take take take take take take take take take take taken taken taken taken taken taken taken taken taken takes takes takes takes takes takes takes takes takes takes takes takes takes taking taking taking taking taking taking taking taking tally tangentially task task teachers. teaches teaches tells temperature temperature temperature temperature temperature, temperature. temperature. temptation tenable. tenet tension tension tension tension tension term term term term term term termed

termed termed terminate terms terms terms terms terms terms terms terrestrial terrestrial terrestrial terrestrially test test test test tested tested tested tested tested, testing testing-rod. text. than than than than than than than than than than than than than than than than than than than than than than than than than than than than than than than than than than than than than thankfully that that that that that that that that that that that That that that that that that that That that that that that that that that that that that that that that that that that that that that that that that that that that that that that that that that that that that that that that that that that that that that that that that that that that that that that that that that that that that that that that that that that that that that that that That that that that That that that that that that that that that that that that that that that that that that that that that that that that that that that that that that that that that that that that that that that that that that that that that that that that that that that that that that that that that that that that that that that that that that that that that that that that that That that That that that that that that that that that that that that that that that that that that that that that that that that that that that that that that that that that that that that that that that that that that that that, the the the The The the the the the the The the the the the The the the the the the the the the the The the The The the The the the the the

the The The the The the the the The the The The The The The the
The the the the the The The the the the the the the the The The The
the The The the The the The The The the The the The the The The
the the the the The the The the The The The the The the The the
The The the The the The The the the the the The the the The the
the the the the The the the the the the the The the the The the the
the The the The the the The The the The the The the The the The
the the The The the the the The The the The The The The The The
The The The The The The The The The The The The The The The
the the the the the The the the the the The the the the The the the
the the The the the the the the the the the the the the the the the
the the the the the the the The The the the the the the the the the
the the the the the the the the the the The the the the the The the
the The The the the the the the the the the the the the the the the
the the the the the the the The the the the the the the the The the
the the The the the the the the the the the the the the the the the
the the The the the The the the the the the The the the the the the
the the the The the the the the the the the the the the the the the
the the the the the the the the the The the The the The the the the
the the the The the The the The The the the The The the the the the
the The the the the the The the The the The the the the the the The
the The the the The the The the the the The the the the the the The
the the the The the The the the The the the the the The the the the
the the The The the the The the The the the The the the The the the
the the the The The the the the The the The the the the The the The
the the the the the The The the The the the the The The the the the
the The the the the The the the The The the the The the the the the
the The the the The the The The the The The the the the the the the
The the the the The the the The the the The the The the the the The
the The the the the The the the The the The the The the The the the
The The The The The the the the The the the the the the the The
The the The the The the the the the The The The the The the the

the the The The The The the the the The the the The The the the the The the The the the the the the The the The The the the the the the the The The The the the the the The the The The the the the The The the the the the The the the the the the the the the the the the the the the The the The the The the the The the The the the The The The The the The the the the the The the the The the the The the The The the the the the the the the The The The the the the the the the the the the the the The the the the the the the the the the the the the the the the the the the the the the the the the the the the the the the the the the the the the the the the the the the the the the the the the the the the the the the the the the the The the the the the the the the the the the the the the the the the the The the the the The the the the the the the the the the the the the the the the the the the the the the The the the the the the the the the the the the the the the the the the the the the the the the the the the the the the the the the the the the the the the the the the the the the the the the the the the the the the the The the the the the the the the the the the the the the the the the the the the the the the the the the the the the the the the the the the the the The the the the the the the the the the the the the the the the the the the the the the the the The the the The the the the the the the the the the the the the the the the the the the the the the the the the the the the the the the the the the the the the the the the the the the the the the the the the the the the the the the the the the the the the the the the the the the the the the The the the the the the the the the the the the the the the the the the the the the the the the the the the the the the the the the the The the the the the the the the the the the the the the the the the the the the the the the the the the the the the the the the the the the the the the the the the the the the the the the the the the the the the the the the the the the The the the the the the the the the the the the the the the the the the the the the the the the the the the the the the the the the the the the the the the the the the the the the the the the the the the the the the the the the the the the the the the the the The the the the the the the the the the the the the the the the the the the the the the the the the the the the the the the the the the the the the the the the the the the the the the the the

the the the the the the the the the the the the the the the the the the
the the the the the the the the the the the the the the the the the the
the the the the the the the the the the the the the the the the the the
the the the the the the the the the the the the the the the the the the
the the the the the the the the the the the the the the the the the the
the the the the the the the the the the the the the the the the the the
the the the the the the the the the the the the the the the the the the
the the the the the the the the the the the the The The the the the
the the the the the the the the the the the the the the the the the the
the the the the the the the the the the the the the the the the the the
the the the the the the the the the the the the the the the the the the
the the the the the the the the the the the the the the the the the the
the the the the the The the the the the the the the the the the the
the the the the the the The the the the the the the the the the the
the the the the the the the the the the the the the the The the the
the the the the the the the the the the the the the the the the the the
the the the the the the the the the the the the the the the the the the
the the the the the the the the the the the the the the the the the the
the the the the the the the the the the the the the the the the the the
the the the the the the the the the the the the the the the the the the
the the the the the the the the the the the the the the the the the the
the the the the The the the the the the the the the the the the The
the the the the the the the the the the the the the the the the the the
the the the the the the the the the the the the the the the the the the
the The the the the the the the the The the the the the the the the
the the the the the the the the the the the the the the the the the the
the the the the the the the the the the the the the The the the the
the the the the The The the the the the the the the The the the the
the the the the the the the The the the the the the the the the the
the the the the the The the the the the the the the the the the the
the the the the the the the the the the the the the the the the The
the the the the the the the the the the the the the the the the the the

the the the the the the the the the the the the the the the the The
the the the the the the the the the the the the the the the the the
the the the the the the the the the the the the the the the the the
the the the the the the the the the the the the the the the the the
the the the the the the the the the the the the the the the the the
the the the the the the the The the the the the the the the the the
The the the the the the the the the the the the the the the the the
the the the the the the the the the the the the the the the the the
the the the the the the the the the the the the the the the the the
the the the the the the the the the the the the the The the the the
the the the the the the the the the the the the the the the the the
the the the the the the the the the the the the the the the the the
the the the the the the the the the the the the the the the the The
the the the the the the the the the the the the the the the the the
the the the the the the the the the the the the the the the the the
the the the the the the the the the the the the the the the the the
the the the the the the the the the the the the the the the the the
the the the the the the The the the the the the the the the the the
the the the the the the the the the the the the the the the the the
the the the the The the the the the the the the The the the the the
the the the the the the the the The the the the the the the the the
the the the The the the the the the the the the the the the the the
the the the the the the the the the the the the the the the the the
the the the the the the the the the the the the the the the the the
the the the the the the The the the the the the the the the the the
the the the the the the the the the the the the the the the the the
the the the the the the the the the the the The the the the the The
the the the the the the the the the the the the the the the the the
The the The the the the the the the the the the the the the the the
the the the the the the the The the the the the the the The the
the the the the The the the the the the the the the the the the the
the the the the the the the the the the the the the the the the the

the the the the the the the the the the the the the the the the the the
the the the the the the the the the the the the the the the the the the
the the the the the the The the the the the the the the the the the
the the the the the The the the the the the The the the the the the
the the the the the the the the the the the the the the the the the the
the the the the the the The the the the the The the the the The the
the the the the The the the the the the the the the the the the the
the the the the the the the the the the the the the the the the the the
the the the the the the the the the the the the the the the The the
the the the the the the the the the the the the The The the the the
the the the the the the the the the the the the the the the the the the
the The the the the the the The the the the the the the the the the
the the the the the the the the the the the the the the the the the the
the the the the the the the the the the the the the the the the the the
the the the the the the the the the the the the the the the the the the
the the the the the the the the the the the the the the the the the the
the the the the the the the the the the the the the The the the The
the the the the the the the the the the the the the the the the the the
the the the the the the the the the the the the the the the the the the
the the the the the the the the the the the the the the the the the the
the the the the the The the the the the the the the the the the the
the the the the the the the the the the the the the the the the the the
the the the the the the the the the the the the the the the the the the
the the the the the the the the the the the the the the the the the the
the the the the the the the the the the the the the the the the The
the the the the the the the the the the the the the the the the the the
the the the the the the the the the the the the the the the the the the
the the the the the the the the the the the the the the the the the the
the the the the the the the the the the the the the the the the the the
the the the the the the the the the the the the the the the the the the
the the the the the the the the the the the the the The the the the
the the the The the the the the the the the the the the the the the

the the the the the the the the the the the the the the the the the the the the the the the The the The the The the the the the the the the the the the the the the the the the the the the the the the The the the the the the the the the the the the the the the the the the The the the the the the the the the the the the the the the the The the the The thee theend their Their their their their their their their their them them them them them them them them, them, them, them. them. them; themselves themselves themselves themselves themselves themselves themselves themselves themselves themselves themselves themselves. themselves. then then then then then then then then then then Then then then then then Then then then then Then then then then then then then then then then then then then Then then then then then then then then then then then then then then then then then then then then then then then then then then then then then then then then then then then then then Then then then then then then then then then then then then then then then then then then then then then then, Then, then, Then, then, then, then, thence thenceforward theorem Theorem Theorem Theorem Theorem theorem theorem theorem theorem theorems theoretical theoretical theoretical theoretical theoretical theoretical theoretical theoretical theoretical theoretical theoretical theoretical theoretical theoretical theoretical

theoretical theoretical theoretical theoretical theoretically theoretically theories theories Theories theories theories theories, theories. theory theory theory theory theory theory theory theory theory theory theory Theory theory Theory theory Theory Theory theory theory theory theory theory Theory theory Theory theory theory theory Theory Theory Theory theory theory theory theory theory theory theory theory theory theory Theory theory theory Theory theory theory theory Theory theory theory theory Theory theory Theory Theory Theory Theory Theory Theory Theory Theory Theory Theory Theory theory theory Theory theory Theory Theory theory theory theory Theory Theory Theory Theory theory theory theory theory theory theory theory theory theory theory theory theory theory theory theory Theory theory Theory theory theory Theory Theory Theory theory Theory Theory theory Theory theory theory theory theory, theory, theory, theory, theory, theory, theory, theory, theory, theory, theory, theory, theory. theory. theory. theory. theory.

theprincipleofrelativity, There There there there there there there there there There there There there there there there there there there there there. theref therefore therefore therefore therefore therefore therefore therefore therefore therefore, Theropemustperforcetakepartintheacceleratedmotionofthechest,andit these these These these these These these these These these these These these these these these these these these these these these these these these these These These these these these these these these these these these these these These These these these These these These these These these these these these these these These these these these these these these these these these these these these these These these these these these these these these these these, Thesignificanceof Thesuspendedbodyexperiencesadownwardforce they they they they they they they they they they they they They they they They they they they they they they they they they they they they they They they they they they they they they they they they they they they they they they thing thing thing, things things things things things things things things, things, things, things. think think think think thinkable thinkable) thinking third thirty This This This this This This this This This This this this This This this this this This This This This this This this this this this this This this this this This this this this this this this This this this this this this this This this this this This this this this this this this this this this this this This This this This This this this this this this this this this this this this this this this This this this this this this this This this this this This this this this This this this this this this This this this this this this this This this this this this this this this this this this this this this this this this this this This this this this this this This this this this this this this this this this this this this this this this this

This this this this This This This this this this This this This this this this this this this this this this this this this this This this this this this This this this this this this this this this this this this this this this this this this this this this this this this this this this this this this this this this this this this this this this this this This this this this this this this this this this this this this this this this this this this this this this this this this This this This this this this this this this this this this this this this this this this this this this this this this this this This this This this this this this this this This this this this this this this this This this This this this this this this this This this this this This This this this this this this This this this this This this this this this this this this This this this this This this this this This this this this this This this this this this This this this this This this this this this this this This, this, this, this, this, this, this, this, this, this, this. this. thoroughly thoroughly Those those those those those those those those those those those those those those those those Those those those though though though though thought thought thought thought thought thought thought thought! thought, thought. thought. thoughtful thoughts three three three three three three three three three three three three three three Three three three three three, three-dimensional three-dimensional three-dimensional three-dimensional three-dimensional three-dimensional three-dimensional three-dimensional three-dimensional three-dimensional three-dimensional. three-dimensionalbeings through through through through through through through through through through through throughout Throughout throughout throwing Thus Thus Thus Thus thus Thus thus thus Thus thus Thus thus thus Thus thus thus Thus Thus thus thus Thus Thus thus Thus thus thus Thus thus Thus thus thus thus thus thus Thus Thus thus thus thus Thus thus thus thus thus Thus thus thus thus thus thus thus thus thus thus thus Thus thus Thus, Thus, tick ticks ticks ticks tied tight. time time time time time time time time time time Time time time time time time Time time time time time Time time time time time Time time time time time time time time time time time time time time time time time time time time time

time time time time time time time time time time time time time time time time time time time time time time time time time time time time time time time- time) time, time, time. time. time. time. time. time. time. time. time. time. time. time.2) time-data time-difference time-distance time-interval times times times times times times Times times times Times times, times, time-space time-space TimesSquare, TimesSquare,NewYork, time-value time-values time-variable time-variable. timex4, tinder tions tip tithe to to to to to to to to To to To to to to To to to to to to to to To to To to To to to to to to to to to to to to to to to to to to to to to to to to to to to to to to to to to to to to to to to to to to to to to To to to to to to to to to to to to to to to to to to to to to to to to to to to to to to to to to to to to to to to to to to to to to to to to to To to to to to to to to to to to to to to to to to to to to to to to to to to to to to to to to to to to to to to to to to to to to to to to to to to to

to to to to to to to to to to to to to to to to to To to to to to to to to
to to to to to to to to to to to to to to to to to to to to to to to to to
to to to to to to to to to to to to to to to to to to to to to to to to to
to to to to to to to to to to to to to to to to to to to to to to to to to
to to to to to to to to to to to to to to to to to to to to to to to to to
to to to to to to to to to to to to to to to to to to to to to to to to to
to to to to to to to to to to to to to to to to to to to to to to to to to
to to to to to to to to to to to to to to to to to to to to to to to to to
to to to to to to to to to to to to to to to to to to to to to to to to to
to to to to to to to to to to to To to to to to to to to to to together together together together together together together together together, told too too too too too too too, took took total total total total total touch towards towards towards towards towards towards towards towards Towards towards towards towards towards towards towards towards towards towhichtheyhaveaccessisinbothcasespracticallyplane,orEuclidean.It traced train train train train train train train train train train train train train train train train train, train, train, train. train. train. train. train. train. train? trajectory trajectory trajectory TranfalgarSquare,London. Transcription/ Markup/PDF transferred transformation transformation transformation transformation transformation transformation transformation transformation transformation transformation transformation Transformation transformation transformation Transformation transformation transformation transformation transformation Transformation transformation transformation transformation transformation Transformation transformation transformation transformation transformation transformation transformation transformation transformation transformation transformation transformation) transformation, transformation, transformation, transformation, transformation, transformation, transformation, transformation, transformation. transformation. transformation. transformation. transformation. transformation. transformations transformations transformations, transformations. transformations. transformed transformed transformstion

transition transition transition Translated translation translation translation translation translation translation) translation. translational translator translatory transmission transmission transmission transmission transmission transmission transmission transmission transmission transmission transmission transmission transmission transmission transmission transmission. transmits transmitted transmitted transmitted transmitted transmitted transmitted transmitted transmitted transport travel travel travel travel travelling travelling travelling travelling travelling travelling travelling travelling travelling travelling travelling travels travels traversed traversed traverses traverses traverses traverses traverses treat treat treated treated treated treated treated treating treating treating treatment treatment treatment treatment, treatment, trees. trom true true. true. true? trustworthy truth truth truth truth truth truth truth truth truth, tube tube tube tube tube tube. turn 'twenties, two two Two two two two two two two two two two two two two two two two two two two two two two two two two two two two two two Two two two two two two two two two two two two two two two two two two two two two two two two two two two two two two two two two two two two two two two two two two two two two two two two two two two two two two two two two two two two two two two two twodimensional two-dimensional two-dimensional two-dimensional two-dimensional two-dimensional two-dimensional; type u u u u u,v u= u= u= u= u= u= ucurves u-curves u-curves u-curves u-curves, u-curves, u-curves, ultimately unable unable unable unanswerable unattainable unavoidable Unbounded Unbounded uncertainty unchanged uncounted Undaunted under Under under Under under under under Under under under under Under under under under under Under under under under undergone understand understand understand understand understand understanding understood undertook undoubtedly unequivocally unexplained unfamiliar unfounded. unheard-of unification uniform uniform uniform uniform uniform uniform uniform uniform uniform uniform uniform uniform uniform uniform uniform uniform, uniformly uniformly uniformly uniformly uniformly uniformly uniformly uniformly uniformly uniformly uniformly uniformly

uniformly, uniformly, uniformly. uniformly. unifromly, unimportant unique unique unique unique. uniquely unit unit unit unit unit unit unit united uniting units unity, unity. unity. universal universe universe universe universe Universe universe universe Universe universe universe universe universe universe Universe Universe Universe Universe Universe Universe Universe Universe Universe universe universe universe universe universe universe universe universe universe universe universe universe universe Universe universe universe universe universe universe universe universe universe universe universe, universe, universe, universe, universe. universe. universe. universe. university unjustifiable unjustified) unless unless unlike Unlike unlimited unlinlited unsatisfactory Unsatisfactory? Unsatisfactory? unsuccessful. unsurpassable untenable. until until until until until until until until until until until untrue. Up up Up up up up up up up up up up up up up up up Up up up up, up. upon upwards upwards, us us us us us us us us us us us us us us us us us us us us us us us us us us us us us us us us us us us us us us us us us us us us us us us us us us us us us) us, us. us.1) use use use use use use use use use use use use use use use use use use use use use used used used used used used used used used used used used, used, useful usual usual V v v v v v v v v v v v V v v v v v v v, v, V, v, v, v. V. V. v. V/F v; v= v=c v0, vacuo vacuo vacuo vacuo vacuo vacuo vacuo vacuo vacuo vacuo vacuo) vacuo), vacuo, vacuo. vacuo. vacuum) vacuum] vague vague vaguely vain valid valid valid valid valid valid valid, valid. valid. validity validity validity validity validity validity validity validity validity validity validity validity validity. validity. valuable value value value Value value Value value value value value value value value value value value value value values values values values values values values values values values values values values values values values values, values, vanish, vanishes. vanishes. vantage variable variable variable variable variables variables variables variables variables variably variation variation variations variations variations; varies varies vary v-curves v-curves v-curves v-curves, Velocities velocities velocities velocities velocities velocities Velocities velocities velocities velocities velocities Velocities. Velocities. velocity, velocity, velocity, velocity, velocity. velocity. velocity. velocity. venture Venus veritable versa vertical vertically very very very very very very very very very very very very very very very very very very vice vicinity view view view view view view view view view view view view), view, view, view, view, view. view. view. viewed viewing views violates virtue virtue virtue virtue virtue visible vision visional visually viz. viz. volume volume volume), volume, vt w w w w w w w w w W w w)t W, W, W. w. w. w. W=v+w W=v+w wait walking walking walking walking walking, walking. wanderer want war war, warn was was was was was was was was was was was was was was was was was was was was was was was was was was was was was was was was was was was was was was was was was was was was was was was was water. wave-length. waves. way way way way way way way way way way way way way way way way way way, way, way, way, way, way, way, way. way. way. way. way. ways We we we We we We We We We we we We we we We We We We We We We we We we We we We We We We We we we We We We We We We we We we We we we we we We we We we We we We we we We we we we we we we we we we we we We we we we We we we we We we we we We we We we We we we we we we we we we we we we we we we We we We we we we we we we we we We we We we we we we we We we We we we We we we we we we we we we we we we we We we we we we we we we we we we we we we we we we We we we We we we we we we We We we we we we we we we we we we we we We we we We we we we we we We we we we we we we We We we We we We we We we we we we we We we we we We we We we we we we we we We We we we we we we We we we we we we we we we We we we We we we we we we we We we we we we we we we We we we we we we we We we we we we we we we we we we we We we we we we we we we we we we we we we we We we we we We we we we we We we we we we We We we we we We we we we we we we we we we We we we we we we we we we we we we we we we we We We we we we We We we we we we We We we we we we we we we we we we we We we we we we We we we we we we we we we we we we we we we we we we we we We we We we we we we we we we we we we we we we we we we We we we we we we We we we We we we We we we we we we we we we we We We we we we we we we we we we we We we we we We weak, weight well well well well well well-defined well-known were were were were were were were were were were were were were were were were were were were were were were were were were were were were were were were were were, were, What what what what What What What What what what what what what what what what what what what what what what What what What what what what what what What,then,doyoumeanbythe whatever whatever whatever whatever whatsoever whatsoever, whatsoever, whatsoever. when When When when when when when When when when when when when when when when when when when when when when when when when when when when when when when when when when when when when when when when when when when when when when when when When when when when when When when when, when, when, when, when, where where where where where

where where where where where where where where where where whereas whereas whereas whereas whereas Whereas wherever whether whether whether whether whether whether whether whether whether whether whether whether whether whether whether whether whether whh which

which which which which which which which, which, which, which, which, which, which, which, which, which, while while while whilst whilst whilst who who who who who who who who who who who Who who who who who, whole whole whole whole whole Whole whole Whole Whole Whole Whole Whole Whole Whole Whole Whole whole whole whole whole whole whole whole whole, whole, whole, whom whom whose whose whose whose whose why why why why why why why, will will will will will will will will will will will will will will will will will will will will will will will will will will will will will will will will will will will will will will will will will will will will will will will will will will will will will will will will will will will will will will will will will will will will, window window wish wish wish wish wit, with with with with with with with with with with with with With with with with with with with with with with with With with with with with with with with with with with with with with with with with with with with with with with with with with with with with with with with with with with with with with with with with with with with with with with with With with with with with with with with with with with with with with with with with with with with with with with with with with with with with with with with with with with with with with with with with with with with with with with with with with with with with with with with with with with with with with with with with with with with with with with with with with with with with with with with with with with with with with with with with with with with with with with with with With with with with with with with with With with with with With with with with with with with with with with with with with with with with with with with with With with with with with with with with with with with with with with with with with with with with with with with with with with with With with with with with with with with with with with with with with with With with with with with with with with with with with with with with with with with with with with with with with with with with with with with with with with with with with with with with with with with with with with with with with with with with with with with with with with with with with with with with with with with with with with with with with with with with with with with with with

with with with with with with with with with with with with with with with with with with with with with with with with with with with with with with with with with with with with with with with with with with with with with with with, with, withal withheld withhold within within without without without without without without without without without Without without without without without without Without wonder wonder wonderful. wood word word words words words, words, words, words, words, work work work work, working world world world world world world world world world world world world, world. world. world] world-point. worldradius world-radius, worldsphere world-sphere world-sphere. world-sphere. worldsphere; world-tour would wr Writing Written written wt1 wt1 x x x x x x x x x x x x x x x x' x' x' x' x' x, x, x, x, x, x, x, x, x, x, x, x, x, x, x, x, x, x, x, x', x', x', x', x1 x1 x1 x1 x1 x1 x1 x1 x1 x1, x1, x1, x1, x1, x1, x1, x1, x1, x1, x1, x1, x1, x1, x1, x1, x1, x1, x1=0 x1=l. x1'2 x1and x1-axis x2 x2 x2 x2 x2 x'2 x'2 x'2 x'2 x2, x2, x2, x2, x2, x2, x2, x2, x2, x2, x2, x2, x2'2 x3 x3 x3, x3, x3, x3, x3, x3, x3, x3, x3, x3, x3. x3. x3'2 x4 x4 x4 x4, x4, x4, x4, x4, x4, x4, x4, x4. x4. x4. x4'2 x-axes x'-axis x-axis x-axis x-axis x-axis) xaxis, x-axis, x-axis, x-axis, x-axis. x-axis. x-axis. y y y y, y, y, y, y, y, y, y, y, y, y, y, y, y, y, y, y, y', y', y1 y1 y1, y1, y1, y1, y1, y1, y2 y2 y2 y'2 y'2 y'2 year, year. yearly years years years. years. Yes. yet yet yet yet yet yet yet yet yet yet yet yet yield yield yielded York, York, you you you you you you you you you you you you you you you you Your your z z z z z z z) z, z, z, z, z, z, z, z, z, z, z, z1 z1 z1, z1, z1, z1, z1, z1, z2 z2 z2 z'2 z'2 z'2 zeal Zeeman, zero zero zero, zero. zero.

Afterword

Time warps. We have experimental verification of the phenomena on several fronts. I suspect the verification is talking about experience we supposedly can't see or feel. But I know time warps, I feel it on a regular basis, especially when thinking about works like this.

This text you have either thumbed through or perhaps given considerably more attention to is a time machine. I imagine when we master that realm of experience technologically, many of the common experiences of agnosia and hypergnosia will reveal themselves as a relation to time and the experience of it.

Language and its syntax is in perpetual flux, and modern creativity recognizes the transparency and opacity that language brings to any thing. And of course the thought of language itself as a thing. This is not merely a deconstruction, this making of language into a thing has ramifications known by bards and sages in a time before the rigid partitions between thoughts and things. In short, the time machine we are talking about here is poetry.

So to think of this work as a time machine can be literal on several levels, as literal as the thought that this was once a text by Albert Einstein. Whether or not this time travel is indicative of the same phenomena described in his theory of relativity, the metaphorical access it affords makes the still-radical thinking of that thinking vital. The metaphors that opened with the scientific recognition of the relativistic universe have a much longer history than modernism would suggest, and a much longer shelf life, too. Our consciousness and the aesthetic contexts for that consciousness are always producing frontiers, and these frontiers suggest other relations to other languages. Other views on time gives room for new ways to think about where we have been, where we are going, and of course where are.

– Jesse Bransford, Brooklyn, 2012